THE
CENTERED
SKIER

A YEAR-OF-THE-TIGER PRODUCTION

THE CENTERED SKIER

by Denise McCluggage

Cover Painting and Illustrations by Bill Brauer

Calligraphy by Al Chung-liang Huang

 **VERMONT CROSSROADS PRESS**

Library of Congress Cataloging in Publication Data
    McCluggage, Denise.
        The Centered Skier.

Bibliography: p.
    1. Skis and skiing.   2. Skis and skiing —
Psychological aspects.   I. Title.
GV854.M2195   796.9'3   76-46301
ISBN 0-915248-09-3

Vermont Crossroads Press,
Box 30,
Waitsfield, Vermont 05673

THANK YOU

Appreciation is due so many.
Here is some for a few dispersed in arbitrary order in unspecifiable amounts.

Ray Montgomery, Editor.

Jack Murphy...Sigi Grottendorfer...Peter Forsthuber...Debbie and
John (Buck) Makowski...Martin Marnett...John Nyhan...
Phyllis Gile Gonzalez...Jim Dodds...Jim Wallace...Steve Fischer...
Ginnie Teague...Beth Chant...Ed Packard...Connie Montgomery...
Heather Newbold...Mia Segal...Beverly Silverman...Janet Lederman...
Ilana Rubenfeld...Gene Coghill...L.V. Brown...John Callahan...Bob Nadeau...
Mike Spino...George Leonard...Chan Weller...Lixi Fortna...Doug Pfeiffer...
John Jerome...Mort Lund...Fred R. Smith...Les Peer... Charlotte Jackson...
Rosi Fortna Harrison...Phil and Penny Northrup Kirk...Damon and
Sara Gadd...Phil and Alma Hill...Barry and Jo Giese Brown...Tom and
Elinor Burnside...Cynthia Miller...Judy Fox...Billy Brauer...Anne and
Ward Just...Dave Sellers...Jean Anwyll...B.J. Anderson...Jean Sherman.

And all the skiers in the Centered Skiing workshops.

This book is for: **Velma F. McCosh McCluggage,** my mother

Al Chung-liang Huang, my *t'ai chi* master

Hathaway, my cat. . . .

. . . . everybody's *t'ai chi* master

CONTENTS

HE, SHE, HIS, HER

A distinct advantage of the Chinese language is that the character *jen* is without gender. It is translated as *man*. It is used to mean, variously: all humankind, a group of people, or an individual person without regard to gender. If one specifically means a *man* as a human male, then one must say so — *nan jen*. Woman is *nü jen*. *T'a* for *he, she,* or *it* is equally genderless.

English, alas, has its genders and its rules of grammar. Within those rules *everyone,* for instance, cannot put on *their* skis. It must be *his* skis or *her* skis or *his or her* skis. I not only find *his or her* ungainly in use, but I bristle at the implication that everywhere it is not used, and *his* appears alone, then that *his* is intended to be exclusively masculine.

Growing up female in the English language, I have refused to be excluded from the word *man* when mankind was meant. Or from *his* or *he* when the words were merely agreeing with an antecedent. To me that use of *his* is a genderless third form that just happens to be the same as the *his* that is also exclusively masculine. When the feminine was meant exclusively other words were used — *she* and *her.*

It did not seem strange to me that the two words, *his* and *his,* were the same. I met stranger things in learning to read. And I found many other words in English that shared appearances and had different meanings. Take *right,* for instance. Was *prerogative* slighted when *direction* was meant? Or *correct,* or *straighten?*

Admittedly, not everyone shared my interpretation. Indeed, in comparing notes I have found few who even understand it. Men, in the human-male meaning, appear mainly to be amused by it. They tend to believe that *his* and *he* are exclusively theirs. I know they are wrong and I refuse the responsibility for their error.

I have written this book in my only language, English, but I have written it in the Chinese sense. I use *man* to be as general as *jen*. When appropriate, I use *him* and *he* and *his* as stripped of gender as *t'a*. I have been as grammatical as I know how, and therefore have used a passel of *his's* and *he's* where I chose not to take refuge in the plural. (The cruelest among you might ask why I did not choose to use *her* and *she* exclusively. I sigh.)

I do not feel excluded by mere pronouns and sincerely trust that no one else will either. But if someone does, I refer him to God. She will explain.

D. McC.

ᡦᡝᠯᠢᠶᠠᠨᠵᠠᡴᠠ

ᡥᠠᡶᠠᠨ

ᡝᡵᡤᡝᠨᡤᡝ

ᠪᠠᠮᠪᡳ

FOREWORD

At Bob Nadeau's *aikido dojo* in San Francisco there is a notice
in the showcase downstairs about when the next classes start.
They don't, the notice says, you just *begin*. This book is like
that. The chapters are numbered progressively, but you can
start anywhere. Wherever you start you should have first read
the chapter that follows anyway.

1

THE EMPTY CUP

Peace begins when expectation ends.
— SRI CHINMOY

Years before I started studying Chinese and *t'ai chi* and collecting Bruce Lee posters, I had a notion that knowing Chinese would help me ski better.

When I announced the idea to chairlift companions and friends it met with blank stares or derision. (I'm ahead of my time, I thought; a favorite refuge when I fail to pipe anyone else into following my parade.) But I was right, though time wandered many paths before returning to this thought. Then out of it evolved the Sugarbush Workshops in Centered Skiing, a new approach—centuries old—to teaching skiing.

It was a success. I skied better, workshop skiers skied better, the workshop instructors skied better. You can ski better.

You need not, unless you have a lifetime to spare, study Chinese to reap these benefits, but you will probably need to readjust some of your thinking. Not a difficult matter, really. It is no more difficult than switching stations on your radio; all the information is already there, waveborne, you simply twist your dial and tune into it.

I had let English, my only language, trap me with its overwhelming linearity. As it marched along, one plonking word after another across one line, then dropped down to plonk along another, it lured my thinking into marching that way, too. In happening one word after another, one line after another, the language beguiled me with its sequentiality. Something was always *following* something by the very nature of the layout. Thus I became fixed on an orderly notion of cause and effect and settled on a simplistic view of time moving along a one-way street.

For me $A + B = C$ meant that if you have A and add B to it you therefore *cause* C, all moving along in an ordered, certain progression. This notion of causality, for all its usefulness in certain circumstances, is not universally applicable. It can, indeed, lead to troubling misconceptions when applied to something so non-linear and all-at-once as skiing. The best you can say about cause and effect in skiing is: Given the *presence* of A and the *presence* of B you will *probably* find C in there, too, somewhere.

My concern over confusing the *simultaneous* and the *sequential* came to me one distant afternoon when I was being taught a now-archaic ski technique that involved rising up and turning the hips. "Rise up and turn the hips," the instructor kept telling me. I kept doing exactly what he said. Then it dawned on me that what he meant was to do both the rising and the turning *at the same time.* I had taken *and* to be a separation in time—do one *and then* do the other.

It was then I decided Chinese would be a better language than English for learning something that involved simultaneity. All I knew about Chinese at the time came from Chinese menus, but I suspected that one pictograph was worth at least 1000 words. I imagined that Chinese characters contained wholes within wholes and meanings interwoven with meanings, thus lessening the risk that the simultaneous would be mistaken for the sequential.

In Chinese characters, I was sure, the energy curls back on itself, forever replenishing itself, rather than bleeding off into vast white margins and dissipating its force. There is a recycling in Chinese, an uninterrupted flow, a regeneration. Chinese, I thought, is more whole, more entire, more...well, *gestalt* (a favorite remnant from my college bout with German). And skiing was all those things, too—whole, entire, gestalt, flowing. Not linear at all, not like English in which I had confined myself.

Therefore, Chinese would help my skiing.*

Not that I dashed off forthwith to pursue the study of Chinese. Many years passed before I found myself with bamboo brush in hand and the tones of Mandarin singing from my record player. By then, skiing was far from my conscious thought. I simply loved the flow and sound of Chinese. Despite hours with earphones and flash cards, I still have only a bowing acquaintance with it. The Chinese language, I have discovered, is very like Chinese food— an hour later and I'd forgotten it all.

Though little was learned, much was learned.

Language, more than being a tool of communication, is a tool of perception. My excursion into Chinese was enough to break some of my confining habits of perceiving, which I had blamed on English. I looked, now, on a different world, or so it seemed.

With English, I had built long hallways and straight thorough-fares, implicit with direction and progression. Chinese widened these passages into chambers, courtyards and gardens draped with willow. They were spacious and directionless.

In my English-built world I looked either to the left or to the right, down these corridors, to the one thing then back to its opposite. They were separated and distant. In the Chinese spaces, polarities wound around on themselves, blending in full view into their opposites. Either/or became both/and—different and the same all at once.

The difference in sameness, the sameness in difference, were not something I had noticed—neck aswivel—in the corridors I had built with English; yet now, in my Chinese spaces, they were simply *there*, like sleeping cats.

In my new spaces I played *t'ai chi ch'uan,* that least martial and most ancient of the Oriental martial arts, a slow moving-meditation done at an underwater pace. And through it my body learned the mingling of "opposites," learned what intellection could not teach: Going out is coming back; rising is falling; stillness is moving; extending is absorbing; dispersing is collecting.

The body learned. The body taught the mind. The body/

---

*Understand, not everyone is so easily enclosed. The great Western scientists, the great skiers, have all managed to transcend the linearity of their alphabetical languages.

mind smiled because it saw *t'ai chi* everywhere. It saw *t'ai chi* in skiing, and skiing in *t'ai chi* and another circle closed.

Embrace tiger, return to mountain... *

BIRTH OF THE WORKSHOPS

I had spent the summer on a beached ferryboat in Sausalito, California, that had once been the home of the late Alan Watts. Al Chung-liang Huang, his friend and collaborator on his last book: *Tao: The Watercourse Way,* taught *t'ai chi,* calligraphy, and Taoist philosophy there that year, and I had steeped in Al's remarkable presence for 10 weeks. I had studied with Al for several years, but never so intensively. That was during the day. Most evenings that summer I spent on the padded mats of Bob Nadeau's *aikido dojo* in San Francisco, further giving myself to an awareness of energy, its flow and its force.

Once back home in Vermont, there were bench marks to measure the changes the summer had made in me. Not changes sought, but changes wrought. I met old circumstances in new ways, more calmly yet more totally at the same time. One such gauge was tennis, a game I came to late in my life and played with more determination than skill. I had not had racket in hand for 3 months, and yet I played better, easier, smoother and enjoyed it more than I ever had.

"What have you been doing?" incredulous cohorts asked.

"*T'ai chi,*" I shrugged.

I began thinking about it,—moving the *t'ai chi* way in sports, being the *t'ai chi* way in sports, teaching sports the *t'ai chi* way, and I was reminded of articles I had written in the late fifties about yoga and Zen in skiing, and recalled my long-ago theory that knowing Chinese would help my skiing.

Now time had ripened.

I was ready then, when Jack Murphy phoned. Jack I had known from the days when I was ski editor of the late *New York Herald Tribune,* and he was manager of Mad River Glen. Now I lived in that same valley within sight of Sugarbush, a ski area he had been instrumental in developing, and of which he was vice president and general manager.

---

*This is the name of a recurring phrase in *t'ai chi ch'uan* and the name of my *t'ai chi* master's first book. (Al Chung-liang Huang, *Embrace Tiger Return to Mountain*). I recommend it.

"I want your thinking," Jack said.

I am always ready with my thinking. (I once had cards printed that read: "Consultant: Any Subject"; ignorance has never been a deterrant.) I am particularly pleased when Jack Murphy asks for my thinking because I have an abiding respect for him. I call him a "street Buddha" because, though he has ranged far from his Bronx origins, a touch of asphalt remains in his wisdom.

Jack wanted my thinking on ski weeks, that perennial package most ski areas have long held out as a bargain enticement to help level the business valleys between weekend peaks. The learn-to-ski-week is a tiger-by-the-tail, yet no single area, unilaterally, dares to give up its ski weeks, or even raise the package price to a profitable level, however much it privately yearns to. It remains as a supermarket loss-leader without a supermarket.

During that summer of my absence, a large, posh tennis camp had opened in Sugarbush Valley, and its throngs of happy— and high-paying—patrons had led Jack to compare these summer weeks with their winter counterparts. Ski weeks came up wanting.

Jack decided it was time to take a critical look at the old package, redesign it, widen its appeal and, he hoped, improve its economics.

Sigi Grottendorfer, the director of the ski school at Sugarbush, just back from his summer job as director of the ski school in Portillo, Chile, was not satisfied with the ski week as it existed, either. He regretted the absence of advanced and expert skiers. He wanted to design a ski week that had something to offer those skiers. He wanted something for the "plateau" skier—the experienced skier who had reached a certain level of proficiency in his skiing and, though stuck there, rarely sought instruction. Sigi had been thinking of a "graduate" level of ski instruction to attract those skiers back to ski school.

And I was high on *t'ai chi* and *aikido* and eager to apply their concepts of Centeredness and energy flow to skiing. Why not *t'ai ski? Ai-ski-do?* The East comes to Eastern skiing!

The three of us met over several lunches and talked, our individual enthusiasms fusing into one. Then Sigi and I worked out an on- and off-slope program for the proposed workshops. The plan: five days, Monday through Friday, with no more than twenty advanced-intermediate to expert skiers: The daily off-slope session will last for an hour or more with energy awareness exercises, body awareness games, and visualization practice. For the on-slope sessions the group will divide into sections, never more than five skiers to an instructor. The morning two-hours on the slope will focus on one particular subject, such as *terrain awareness, the pole plant, turn initiation, carving.* The skiers will be video taped in the morning and the tapes played back and discussed during lunch. For the two-hour afternoon session, each section will move on to another instructor and another focus.

In our planning sessions I was delighted by the way Sigi took to the "new" vocabulary—Center, *ch'i,* flow; but then he had grown up in Austria speaking German and had learned English and Spanish well. Why should a handful of new words be difficult? The words, of course, were more than words; they were the symbols of a simpler way of perceiving how skiing happened, and how to let it happen. Sigi recognized that and welcomed it. He was receptive because the words fit what *he was already doing.* He was moving from his Center on skis. He was relating to the mountain. He was ever seeking the simpler way—the *more* in the *less.* And his energy flowed, unimpeded by tension, along the simpler lines he made of his long legs and arms. It fed the stillness of his upper body. He was a Centered Skier before the term existed.

Now here were words for the act; here was a philosophy for the actuality. He was delighted, too. We scheduled the first Sugarbush Workshop in Centered Skiing for the week before Christmas, 1975. The ads bragged, "In 5 years everyone will be teaching skiing this way; this year Sugarbush is the only one."

Jack Murphy quipped: "We don't teach the *comma* position. We teach the *karma* position."*

The bimonthly workshops begin. With each new Monday morning I find the air in the room patterned with expectations. As the season progressed many students had read or heard enthusiastic comments about the program before they arrived, and they flew their hopes like banners. Others wore the folded look of doubt. And some silently threw down a challenge: This better be worth the 250 clams. Or: Just try and mess with *my* mind.

---

*The Centered Skiing workshops were an addition to the regular ski week program, not a replacement. The "improved economics" were relative. Although the workshops were priced four or five times higher than other ski weeks, they also *cost* much more to do; the instructor-to-student ratio was held at 1 to 4; there were 5 to 6 hours of instruction on the slope and off, daily videotaping, lunch and lifts. Still, the ceiling had been breached and many other areas followed suit in repricing and redesigning their ski weeks.

To clear the room of this atmospheric clutter I ask the assembled skiers to sit quietly for a moment and look inside themselves discovering if they have any *expectations,* any preconceived notions about what might happen. I ask them to collect these expectations, put them in an envelope (we start early with visualization), and seal it and label it: *Expectations.* "Now while you're at it, visualize a bonfire in the center of the room and feed your envelope to the flames." Together (I usually find I'm harboring expectations, too) we watch the envelopes blacken and curl and the expectations go up in smoke. I see some half-smiles around the room; a sense of relief, I suspect. Expectations, whether they are your own or someone else's *for* you, are burdening.

Now, with the cooling ashes before us, we are ready to *experience directly* what ever happens rather than being limited by a scenario. Burn the script; it's ad lib time.

Expectations, even when realized, are limiting. "Just let happen what happens,' I suggest to the workshop skiers. "Why go home with a perfect right turn when you might go home knowing how to fly."

Expectations are also the surest road to disappointment. For instance, if you have arrived Friday night in a gentle piling of new snow and you awake Saturday morning to a shroud of fog and the distant sound of dripping, you are disappointed. You are now faced with two immediate choices. Stay disappointed—grouse all day, mutter on the lift, complain during lunch, sharpen the edges of your sarcasm, and generally revel in your misery. *Or* recognize that it is your *attachment* to your expectation, to what you wished for, that has soured your view of the world. If the fog is, the fog *is.* There is no intent in it. Nothing personal is meant. Your personal cloud of gray will not affect it one whit. Your disappointment will only feed your insistence on being disappointed. It will only underscore the contrast between the day you had in mind and the day that is—The contrast between *desire* and *actuality.*

Your disappointment lies in the mismatch.

Should you, then, put on your Pollyanna hat and up parasol? Should you pretend that the day is blest with sun, and the snow is cornstarch and not mashed potatoes? If you do that, there is a mismatch between *pretense* and *actuality.*

There is no need to *pretend* anything because there already is an *is.* If you want what *is* you have a match and there is no room for disappointment.

Ski in the eternal *now* in the ever-present *here*. That's all there is, anyway. And when you do ski here/now the positive in the negative reveals itself and the gates of all mysteries slide open. (If you don't *expect* them to, of course).

During one workshop held precariously late in the season we were visited by all 57 catalogued varieties of Vermont weather. Unseasonable warmth with slush and rain yielded to unseasonable cold with the icy conditions known locally as "loud powder." Then the week closed with a yellow sun smiling on a new fall of fluff. While many other skiers moaned about their fate as they alternately squished or scratched their way down the mountainside, the workshop skiers were having a ball. "Tell me, honestly. Do you brainwash 'em?" an onlooker asked me behind his hand.

Same weather, same snow for all, but the miserable skiers were miserable because they were *stuck* on the difference between what they expected and what they got; the workshop skiers simply skied on what was there because it was there.

I ask the reader, now, to do what I ask the skiers to do at the beginning of the workshop. Collect your expectations and consign them to a bonfire. This book may not be the book you expected; it may not be the book I expected to write. It is the book that *is*. As the late Bruce Lee said, and the earlier Lao Tzu, "The value of a cup is in its emptiness."

2

CENTERING
AND
ENERGY

...Except for the point, the still point
There would be no dance....   — T.S. ELIOT

Man is the center of his own universe. Individually Ptolemaic, he is at the hub of all he surveys. *Front* and *back, right* and *left, up* and *down* are all differentiations based on that perception made about the space in which he moves. There is no universal *front,* no immutable *up.*

Man can use this notion of his centrality either to *separate* himself from everything or to *relate* to everything. Either: what is front to me is back to you; we have nothing in common. Or: my left is your right; let us join hands and celebrate our sharing.

There is a cultural bias in the Western world toward separation, toward one *or* the other, the disconnected, the discrete, the *me* or the *you.* ("Remember, we're all in this alone," Lily Tomlin says.) But physics, which has provided us with the metaphor for that aloneness, that ultimate separateness, with its model of the atom, is now ahem-ing over in the corner. Maybe things are not quite so separate, after all. Particles are, it seems, not exactly particles at that. All the thingness-apart is being stirred by the new physics into a jelly mass of oneness. Well, not exactly oneness either, more—how are you going to explain this—of bothness. Both particle and wave, both unique and the same, both many and one. Even that is only what they seem to be, not what they are.

Buddha smiles; Taoists play their t'ai chi; in the Shaolin temple another "grasshoppa" is struck by a chunk of firewood— and enlightment; Zen masters arrange flowers, serve tea. So what else is new?

In skiing, the bias toward separateness is a barrier that blocks growth. To move smoothly and efficiently in space it is necessary to be sensitive to relationships—relationships of spaces to spaces, their shifting and flowing—and to go with the flow.

Look at skiers. What is the essential difference between a good skier and a poor skier, between the ones who gladden the eye and delight the soul and the ones who jangle the aesthetic nerves? It is their relationship with the mountain.

The poor skiers fight the mountain, attacking it with their tiny poles, their miniature spirits, and slashing at it with their edges. The good skiers join the mountain, commune with it, go with it. Yes, their poles stab and their edges cut, but with a difference. The difference is that the poor skiers have an I-It relationship with the mountain, to use Martin Buber's term. The mountain is a thing apart from them, an object to be manipulated and subdued. The good skiers have an I-Thou relationship with the mountain; there is union.

In ski racing much is made of attack. Attack the course, attack the mountain. But watch the experts of aggressive skiing, such as Gustavo Thoeni or Ingemar Stenmark. On their best runs they are not attacking the mountain, but attacking with the mountain. They have caught the energy wave. Contrast such a run with another when they are slightly out of phase, struggling to attain the crest. The struggle can be mistaken for attack, and often is by television commentators, but the electronic timer reveals the truth. There is a subtle difference measured in important hundredths of seconds between competing with the mountain and competing with the mountain. Competitors who have experienced those transcendent moments when they have ridden the energy wave understand.

It is exciting to see the change in the workshop skiers

when their bias toward separateness begins to yield to one of relating. ("The mountain is your brother.") The difference is made obvious by a comparison of the videotapes taken the last day with those made on the first day. It is a small but critical difference. The skiers no longer look as if they were superimposed on the mountainside with the background a poor process-shot from a low-budget movie. They have joined the mountain. There is a kinship.

In Chuang Tzu there is a story of Prince Wen-hui's cook, a master at carving an ox with the dancing blade of his knife. He does not attack the carcass, he goes with its grain, letting his knife be guided into the yielding places, never striking bones and tendons that might dull his blade. "A good cook changes his knife once a year, because he *cuts*," Cook Ting explains. "A mediocre cook changes his knife every month because he *hacks*. I have had this knife 19 years and have cut up thousands of oxen with it, yet its edge is as keen as if it just came from the grindstone."

I think of the prince's cook as I watch John Nyhan, one of our workshop instructors, ski. He is similarly sensitive to the yielding places of the mountain, and his edges remain sharp long after most of us have nicked and burred ours with hacking. John carves the mountain like Cook Ting carves an ox, and, like the prince, I learn a lesson in living as I watch.

THE ENERGY CONNECTION

We are more than physical beings, more than flesh-and-bone units wandering at random over an alien landscape; we are *energy beings* as well, moving in a field of forces in which all things, from the smallest flower to the most distant star, are related. Modern physics is coming to an awareness of that interrelationship; some ancient philosophies have always recognized it. In many of them we are believed to relate to those things near and far, to the spaces we are in and the spaces within us, through our Center. Our Center is considered the place through which we connect with the energies of the universe.

Just below the navel is an area. Some say it is a point. Some measure its precise location by lengths of the thumb joint— 1½ or 2—but those who measure are the ones who count angels on the heads of pins. The Japanese call the place *hara,* the Chinese call it *tan t'ien,* the Sufi term is *kath,* and for yogis it is the *third chakra*. We could call it CG because it is, more or less, the body's center of gravity. Think of it as CG if you want to, or think of it as a center of consciousness, a center of connectedness, or simply as the Center.

Put your hand there now, just below the belt, where you might pat a satisfying meal or feel for the kicking evidence of new life. Put your hand there, cupping the swell of your breath as you breathe deep into your belly. Be aware of that place. You

can think as you choose of that centerpoint of your body—it can be for you something merely physical, something metaphysical, or something metaphorical. It does not really matter how you *think* of it; your growing *awareness* of it is all that is needed for Centered Skiing.

In our Western world the head is generally accepted as the seat of our consciousness. We place it just below the roof of our skull and a few inches behind the eyes. There at *head*quarters a tiny driver seems to sit, manipulating controls as if the body were a giant steam shovel. The driver rotates the cab to survey the scene and more or less skillfully lifts, retracts, and extends the limbs. What many of us separate out to call *I* lives in that spot. Perhaps that's why so many of us walk around leading with the head, leaving the body trailing behind like smoke.

Why should consciousness be located in the head any more

than anywhere else? Maybe because the brain and all the tele-ceptors — eyes, ears, nose — are there. That is, actually, as accept-able a reason as any. Consciousness, after all, is a relationship and has no physical location except as we *choose* to locate it. If we decide to house our consciousness in the penthouse, fine, but we must realize that it is living there simply because we prefer to put it there. If we choose to relocate it, we can — wherever and whenever we want. Consider the sports cliché: "He has the good hands." After all it is wise for a ballplayer to put his con-sciousness in his hands.

Our prevalent choice of locating consciousness in the head complicates proper use of the body. Efficient movement originates in the Center. That's where the major muscles are attached to the pelvis and that's where movement begins. (See Chapters 5 and 6.) Watch fine athletes move; keep your eyes on their Centers, at the core of their physical being. Watch them lay their moves from Center. Those who move with ease and effectiveness administer their moves from Center. Their peripheral muscles are clerks.

That is why you as a skier should choose to locate your consciousness at your Center. Skiing is movement. Centered Ski-ing is efficient movement, which means being Centered over your skis, Centered in your being and doing, and Centered in your en-vironment. Centered Skiing is skiing in balance, and in harmony of movement, emotion, and thought.

In the workshops, I have the skiers get a clearer notion of moving from Center by asking them to grasp a handful of their clothing at that spot over their lower abdomen, or take hold of a low belt buckle, and propel themselves around the room. With their hands at their Center they pull themselves forward, push themselves back, and tug themselves to the side. All movement is sensed as originating from their Center. The head rides the shoulders like a falcon and does not lead the way.

Soon there's a surge of energy in the room. It's a small change and some do not notice it, but we are moving with less effort. We have connected with a larger force. We are moving about the room like bumper cars at the amusement park, gliding along as if we had plugged into an exterior energy source. Not everyone is comfortable with the feeling, not yet.

Stand-Off

We play games to enhance the sense of Center, and to understand how relocating consciousness to the midpoint helps skiing. One such game is called Stand-Off. I learned it from my friend George Leonard, author of *The Ultimate Athlete,* whose black belt in *aikido* and association with the New Games movement have far from dulled his old-fashioned competitive edge.

The game: Choose a partner, preferably one near your own height. Stand facing each other. If you have the shorter arms, establish the proper distance by touching your hands to your partner's shoulders. Both of you must have your feet *together* and keep them that way. If you move them, you've lost.

Put your hands up with your palms facing those of your partner, patty-cake style. You win if you can make the other person lose balance—either falling backwards or forwards—by contacting the other's palms, and *only* palms, with yours. If you both lose balance, you both lose.

In the workshop, the games end quickly at first. Some wild lunges connect and bodies start to fall from the heels, like timber. Then the learning begins. The next time the aggressors strike they hit only thin air and teeter into their partners. The players rooting themselves to the floor with sheer determination discover that the shock of a blow breaks them off at the floor as if they were frozen reeds.

Soon the games lengthen as the players learn to *absorb* the attacking energy, yielding and bouncing back, like a pine branch releasing a weight of snow. The entire body begins to reflect that yielding wave. Instead of a resistant, poker-stiff body that can do nothing but transmit directly to the feet any shock applied to the hands, there is now a giving in the arms and shoulders, a receptivity in the trunk, and a flexion in the knees. This way, the attacking energy is spread evenly, and its power to displace the body is dissipated.

Your Center is the key. As the arms move back, the lower body eases forward. The force intended to knock you backward is accepted by your Center and redirected downward, through the flexing knees and the receptive feet into the ground. The energy that was meant to displace your body has actually made it more secure. It is the way of those martial arts in which attacking energy is not resisted but is accepted and turned into an asset. In Stand-Off, if the acceptance is not complete, if the arms are stiff or if the thighs grab—or even if there is holding on with the toes— the rechanneling of the energy flow is blocked, and you totter.

Stand-Off can teach your body in a few minutes more about skiing than you can learn in hours on the slopes. Look how you are standing for the game; you could be on skis—knees flexed, upper body erect, hands forward. It is the General Position for skiing with one exception—your clamped-together feet. Modern skiing is much more lax in its demands for feet-together skiing (see Chapter 12).

When you are actually skiing, you are playing a cosmic game of Stand-Off. As you hit bumps or run across variable snow conditions you encounter forces capable of knocking you off balance. If you meet these forces with a firm resolve and a tense resistance you may well *be* knocked off balance. You lose the game. But if you go with the energy, if you absorb it, soothing any disruptive influences into usefulness just as you do in your winning games of Stand-Off, you will ride out whatever the mountain has to offer, and in style.

For those who want to explore this game's lessons in energy dynamics even further, there is George Leonard's *aikido* version of Stand-Off, in which you keep your palms in constant contact with your partner's and both close your eyes.

Jump on My Boat

A small and perfect pond lies across the road from an old Cat-skill resort hotel where I first started the study of *t'ai chi* with Al Chung-liang Huang. On the pond floats a chunk of styrofoam about the size and shape of a large surfboard. A teaching game evolved out of the chance presence of that piece of buoyancy. A person would stand at one end of it and another would jump on the other end. As with Stand-Off, the absorption—or nonabsorption—of the newly applied energy was instantly obvious. Those who were wet had clearly resisted the new forces that had come into their space and were projected into the pond. Those who took the forces to their Center, going with the energy and absorbing the bobbing in their knees and body, rode out the crisis.

The nice thing about Jump on My Boat is that there is no need to have a pond or a boat to play it. You can conjure them up. In the Centered Skiing workshops we do just that, and we hop on each other's boats, sensing the energy, absorbing it in the flexion of the knees, the give of the body, and the stillness of the Center.

Not all the workshop skiers immediately appreciate the

game's applicability to skiing—there are some incredulous looks—but most come to understand that skiing into a mogul field is the same as a whole gang of boat jumpers coming at you at once. When someone jumps on your boat you *absorb* the energy in your knees as your end of the craft pops up, and then *extend* with it as it hollows out. The cue for your knees comes from the boat. Similarly, the moguls give the cue to your knees as to when and how much they rise, and how quickly they drop to maintain the firm contact with the surface of the snow. With the boat, as with the bumps, the small flexing of the ankles expresses the fineness of that contact—the toes dropping, for instance, to keep your feet in touch with the boat. Or to keep your skis following the contour of the moguls.

With neither the boat nor the bumps are there preconceived notions; no instructions from *head*quarters. Unhook your body from the tightening reins of thought and go with the boat and the bumps. Your knees know how; your Center can tell. Let them.

CH'I

In a workshop in Centered Golf, I had the group do an exercise in energy awareness in which they reached quietly into inner spaces. One participant, a woman who spends large amounts of time and money in determined pursuit of any sport she undertakes, didn't like it. With one hand on cocked hip and the other outthrust, she complained, "I don't find this energizing at all! I feel all relaxed and—*blah*."

She had limited her understanding of energy to a snap-crackle-pop idea of it. To her, energy meant what we used to call *pep,* or a get-things-done nervous activity that many people who live their lives in a controlling mode—manipulating things, events, people, and themselves—identify as energy. No wonder the prevailing fault in her golf game was spinning her shoulder to start the downswing in her rush to be effective, to manipulate the ball. Such goal-fixated effort is out of synchronization with the natural rhythm of the energy wave. It rides ahead of it or behind it, relying on *force* instead of the smooth power of *ch'i.*

The forceful way is successful often enough to account for its popularity, but it has all the built-in limitations and penalties of excessive effort.* A surer and more lasting way of doing is to

---

*Chapters 4 and 5.

tune into the energy of the universe, sense its flow, and catch its wave at the crest. To do that you need the sense of connectedness and collectedness referred to in this book as Centeredness.

Being *energized* does not necessarily mean being *energetic,* although that can be part of it. Energy has its *yin* side, too, its

calm as well as its storm. Being energized is simply being connected. It is being relaxed and receptive, though not collapsed and dull. It is better described as *relaxed/alert.* For a person unfamiliar with the relaxed/alert state, particularly for one coming from habitual tension, a first meeting could be experienced as *blah,* rather like the desert can be experienced as empty until our sensibilities are attuned to its subtle variety. Exploration of that *blah* space, without expectations or preconceived notions, will

reveal it to be a highly *potential* state, a state infinite with all possibilities—action, rest, contemplation, laughter. Each is capable of
being experienced wholly; *ch'i* feeds the fullness of its potential.

But what is *ch'i*, or *ki*, as the Japanese call it?* It is called
by many names—*pranha* and *élan vital* for instance—but what
it is remains as essentially unanswerable as a similar question in
music: What is soul? Soul, like *ch'i*, defies definition but, like *ch'i*,
its presence or absence is instantly noticeable. (As in: "It got no
soul, man!" in which soul is pronounced with at least four syllables.)

☯

Ch'i, too, is a property of movement, of art, and of individual expression. It is everlasting. It is a calling card that says
the breath of life was here, and remains here though suspended
in the stillness of time. The brush calligraphy that dances through
these pages is full of *ch'i*, not only the *ch'i* of Al Chung-liang
Huang whose brush made the marks, but the *ch'i* of the ancients
who made similar marks at Lan T'ing, the Orchid Pavillion by the
water lilies, where they gathered with cups of wine, bamboo music,
and bamboo brushes to loose and capture their *ch'i* on long scrolls.

Thus is *ch'i* the expression of life's continuity, the evidence
of one ongoing energy expressed in a myriad ways. Skiers express
ch'i, too. Sustained by the breath of the universe, they leave their
marks on the mountain scroll. They connect and unify, they parti-
cularize and specify. They are calligraphers, too.

---

*The Chinese character that is usually translated as *energy* is commonly
romanized as *ch'i* (Pronounced *chee* in a sharply falling tone). The same
character is called *ki* (key) in Japanese—as in *aikido*. The apostrophe in
ch'i is important. It signals the aspirated initial *chuh* sound. Without the
apostrophe, as in the *chi* of *t'ai chi,* the sound is an unaspirated soft
gee. Chi is an entirely different word from *ch'i*. The apostrophe also
signals a hard sound in *t'ai* so that *t'ai chi* is pronounced *tye jee* (a
falling tone followed by a high, level tone.)

A common error is the use of *ki* as if it were a physical place—
the solar plexus, or the Center—rather than the *energy* flowing from (and
to) the Center. The Center is not *ki;* it is *hara* in Japanese and *tan t'ien*
(don tea-n) in Chinese. (All pronunciations here are Mandarin.)

As long as we are being phonetic, *tao,* which is sometimes translated as the path or the way, is pronounced in Chinese as *dow* (falling
tone) as in Jones. In Japanese the same character is *do* (between *daw*
and *dough* when spoken) again, as in *aikido*.

And while we are at it, *kung fu* is pronounced as if it started
with a hard gee, and *I Ching* sounds like *yih jing*. Don't blame Chinese;
blame the scholars who converted the sounds of its brush strokes into
Roman letters. Or, better yet, as it says in the *I Ching,* "no blame."

Ch'i cannot be defined, then, but it can be sensed, felt, seen, and demonstrated. Perhaps it can be photographed, if one is to take the swirls of color surrounding fingertips, torn leaves, and other subjects of Kirlian photography as a manifestation of this energy. Some people routinely *see* such colors and coronas in everyday life. They claim they can judge the health and mood of a person by the color and size of this aura surrounding them. Anger, it seems, *is* red, and not just metaphorically so.

Auras are probably always there but usually unseen like so much other information to which our senses are not habitually, or culturally, attuned. In some cultures people hear jungle drums over extraordinarily long distances; in others, apparent telepathy is commonplace, and in our own, some people — usually women — are allowed the authenticity of their hunches more than others are. I suspect that children commonly see auras, but soon learn to ignore them because so little is made of them in their world. Ignored, they disappear.

My first experience with *seeing* energy was at Esalen Institute, in Big Sur, California, where I had gone to take a workshop with Bob Nadeau, an extraordinary former policeman who has become a teacher, a *sensei,* in the Oriental sense. Among the things he teaches are meditation, energy awareness, and *aikido.*

In the workshop, I was one of some 20 people sitting in a circle in a room, hands joined and eyes closed, attending to our breathing and being aware of our Centers. Then Bob asked us to open our eyes and look at the person directly across from us. I was instantly aware of a white light rapidly circling our group (I was reminded of the tigers whirling themselves into butter in the Little Black Sambo story from my childhood). Bob was directly across from me; as I looked at him I saw his eyeglasses suddenly blanked with ultraviolet, as opaquely purple as welder's goggles. A neon yellow line traced his head and shoulders. Radiating out from that was the same ultraviolet that filled his glasses and X'd across his chest.

Wow! My eyes popped; I looked harder, and all disappeared. It was just a room again, and people, not butter, and Bob with clear glasses, so I returned my attention to my breathing and to my Center: the brilliance instantly reappeared. Again I *looked* at it, and again it disappeared. Then I played sidling-up-to-it games, pretending not to look — mentally whistling and sneaking glances. It came and went, dependent entirely on whether or not I was *trying* to see it. The trying turned it off, the allowing let it be.

It had several phases: the happenstance allowing, and the trying to allow; the looking that didn't work, and the *seeing* that just happened.

I thought; some people see like that all the time; they watch molecules collide and it is *energy* they are seeing, pure $E = mc^2$ stuff. I accepted that I was not one of those so blessed, and presto, I was blessed for another moment. Tricky!

I was not in Bob Nadeau's presence until 5 years later, at another Esalen workshop. This time I simply allowed him to swim in a constant mist of ultraviolet. No gee whiz, no wow, and no disappearing act.

When I'm in the same receptive mode I can sometimes see other manifestations of energy. I see dam-like dark areas in people's bodies, which I take to be energy blocks. I see them so clearly at times I feel pressed to do something about them, just as I might want to straighten a picture in someone's hallway, or move a log in the fireplace just enough to create a proper draft to burn well. Perhaps fortunately, the urge is rare, and only with people I know.

At a party one night I walked across the room to push my finger into the upper shoulder of a psychiatrist friend of mine. His arm dropped about 2 inches. He was surprised. "How did you know that's my tension spot?" he asked. I was surprised he was surprised. "I saw the energy block." He is a brilliant but rational man, and scoffs at the notion of visible energy. I quote R.G.H. Siu to him: "...to judge something that lies beyond reason by means of reason itself does not appear reasonable." He is not listening; "Shut up and massage." He is also a funny man.

A few years ago I saw a basketball game that was a fascinating network of visible energy, thanks perhaps in equal parts to my squinting eyesight and to an intervening haze between my seat and the playing floor; I seemed to be supporting the roof of the Oakland Colliseum with my neck. Bright cords of varying width connected the Golden State Warriors at their middles. The lines all emanated from Rick Barry, making him look like something straight out of Castaneda. Rick was glowingly, obviously, the hub of the team that night. The changing thicknesses of the cords extending from him indicated where his next pass was going, even when he was looking in another direction. The ball followed a remarkably predictable path down shining corridors of energy.

In contrast, the New York Knicks, the evening's visitors, were disconnected. A few feeble lines extended from Bill Bradley to two other teammates, but Walt Frazier moved in his own cocoon, and Spencer Haywood, too, played in noble isolation. Predictably, the score was lopsidedly in the Warriors' favor. So much so, indeed, that some might have called it a dull game, but for me it was worth every dime of the scalper's price.

At the only other basketball game I've seen live in recent years, this one at Madison Square Garden, the energy lines were only spasmodically visible—perhaps I was *trying* to see them—but Pete Maravich was a show by himself. He appeared as an octopus of light with bright tentacles reaching outward, only rarely finding another energy to connect with. No wonder his dazzling passes so often went untouched into the crowd; his virtuoso displays of ball handling were the gleaming jugglings of his own energy field.

I think many coaches and players of all sports *see* energy paths, or certainly sense them, and respond to them without having to understand or explain why. Later they sometimes clothe their experiences in acceptable rationality for the press—and for themselves—rather like someone justifying his compliance with a posthypnotic suggestion. ("I scratched my elbow just then because it itched.")

Maybe coaches and players would be more consistently effective if they accepted the concept of an *energy flow* that can be sensed and seen. They could then intentionally develop those powers of *knowing* that are outside the culturally accepted means of cognition. *Seeing* an energy gap in a defense, for instance, is as valid as noticing that a player took a long time to get up after the last play. The physical is part of it, but it is not all of it. The energy, the *ch'i,* is the rest of it.

Imagine the possibilities if players granted their intuition full partnership with their reason and allowed themselves to *see* energy, to trust their sensing of it. If they worked on developing an awareness of energy flow as much as they work on the physical aspects of their sport they might really get their game together. How valuable to know when the blitz is coming, where the pass is going, who is yielding and who is staying, who is connected with himself today and who is not. The information is all there; it is just a matter of recognizing it. The best of the players do it already, of course, particularly on certain golden days. They don't talk about it. Some don't even think about it for fear they might lose it—whatever it is.

Ski racers sense energy flow, too. Some see it as a bright track limning their line. When they see it they know that what they have to do is launch themselves into it, like a kayak into a swift stream, and see to it that they remain pointing most advantageously and stay with the current. They ride it thus. Such days are not common, but they are never forgotten.

Becoming aware of energy flow is not hard, although using it well takes experience and practice. In the Centered Skiing workshops we begin our awareness exercise by taking partners and standing face to face with our hands held out parallel to the floor. One palm is facing upward and the other downward. We stand with our palm-up hands directly under the palm-down hands of our partners leaving 3 or 4 inches of space between. Standing thus we scan our bodies for the tension of expectation and allow it to ease. We attend to our breath, following it to our Center. Then we let happen what happens.

"Hey, my hand's getting hot!" someone says. "Mine's tingling," someone else says. "We've got an electric current going here," says another. Some look puzzled, or left out, as if they hadn't yet been chosen for a team. Those who feel this force in their hands play with it, pulling it like taffy, sometimes stretching it far across the room. After 5 or 10 minutes, we change partners. The rest of the group begins to feel it, now, too; some decide to "explain" it—group suggestibility, self-hypnosis, metabolism. That's all right, but meaningless. Even naming it is meaningless; but we call it *ch'i*.

The Unbendable Arm

Having felt the something we call *ch'i* we go on in the workshops to put it to use. We begin with the classical exercise from *aikido* often called The Unbendable Arm. The exercise demonstrates that the relaxed/alert state of Centeredness with *ch'i* extending is stronger than purposive muscularity.

You need a partner for this exercise. Stand in an easy manner, legs about hip-width apart and extend either arm at shoulder height in front of you. Your elbow is not locked nor is it bent, but rather your arm lies in a natural curve with the hand open and the fingers relaxed as if you have just thrown a ball.

Your partner will try to bend your arm, perhaps by resting your hand on his own shoulder and bringing both of his hands to bear at your elbow, or by putting one hand on your upper arm and the other at your wrist. Either way, he exerts all the force that he finds necessary.

If you remain Centered and keep your *ch'i* flowing, your partner will find your arm virtually unbendable. If, however, you yield to the habit of resisting with muscle power, a small tussle will ensue, and your arm will be more easily bent.

One of several mental images can maintain the unbendability of your arm. One is to see your arm as a fire hose and your *ch'i,* originating in your Center, as an unending stream flowing through it keeping it firm. Another is to lengthen your arm in your imagination, sending it visually out through the wall well into the hills where your fingers become entwined with the trees. Another is to visualize a plaster cast of energy encasing your physical arm. Or you can see an arm existing unbent and unbendable in space before you; you merely join it with your physical arm and merge the two in solidarity.

Any similar image will work if you will let it, but often images burst like soap bubbles as soon as someone touches you to test your arm's unbendability. Your muscles tighten almost involuntarily and the localized resistance begins. Such resistance is self-defeating for your muscles as well as in its sudden blockage of *ch'i.* When you tense for the resistance you are contracting your biceps, a flexor whose job it is to close the elbow, the very thing you wish to avoid. You are, then, trying both to flex your arm and keep it extended. The additional force applied by your partner soon tips the balance; your arm bends.*

Sometimes in our workshops the ones with the greatest strength, usually men, have the most trouble finding their unbendable arm. Their life is a record of success using muscular strength, and they are reluctant to give it up for an unknown. Women, with less out-and-out physical strength on which to rely, are better acquainted with the inherent power of *yin* energy. They often find their unbendable arm on the first try.

Partners should approach those who are having trouble finding their unbendable arm as they would an easily spooked horse whose hide quivers at a touch: gently, speaking softly, and taking time between moves. When you put your hand on your partner's upper arm, say, "I am giving you more energy; accept it. Do not resist it." Feel the muscle relax again under your hand,

---

*George Leonard, in his book *The Ultimate Athlete* and in his workshops, gives more exercises for experiencing your energy body. Classes in *aikido* and some of the less macho of the martial arts can also introduce you to it properly.

watch for the breath to go back to Center; then put your other hand to your partner's wrist and say, "This is not a threat. This is more energy; use it to make your arm firmer."

Then slowly break his arm. Actually, stop well short of that. The lessons of The Unbendable Arm can be learned without mayhem.

If you or your partner cannot find the unbendable arm right away, let it go and come back later. It will be there. In the workshops nearly everyone experiences the unbendability of his arm sooner or later, and derives an experiential understanding that *there is more real strength in being attentively relaxed than there is in resistive effort.*

We transfer the lesson to the ski slope. Let the arms holding your poles ride like reeds floating on a pond. As energy arms they are untiring, untireable. Let the energy course through your legs. Let them be receptive and yielding to changes in the terrain, yet as strong as your unbendable arm. Their power comes from their ability to accept the bumps. Without resisting they resist. Muscularity is not strong enough; it is wearing and self-limiting. In ch'i is the real force, not in forcefulness.

As you ski, check yourself to see if you make automatic muscular reactions, tensing to a change in snow texture or terrain as if it were your partner's hand on your arm. If you do, attend to your breathing. Extend your ch'i; let it flow outward and return through your Center. Sense your connectedness.

If you are a coach, you would do well to scan your skiers for energy breaks and blocks, for kinks in their ch'i. Watch them in a receptive mode, eyes soft rather than looking sharply; let their images play on a larger retina. *Sense* with all your perceptors and inhale the *feel* of their skiing rather than looking for picture-perfect positions. They can look as if they came straight off the cover of the how-to book, but if their skiing is without ch'i, it is without life.

3

THE
ONE AND
ITS OTHER

This is this, this is also that.
— CHUANG TZU

Active and passive, high and low, positive and negative, good and evil: We call them opposites and with the very word arm their camps and set them in conflict, in *opposition.* If linguist Benjamin Lee Whorf is correct, if our language is a "vast pattern-system" that organizes not only how a person communicates but how he "builds his house of consciousness," then we have an automatic adversary relationship between every pair of opposites in English.

What has this to do with skiing? Consider the chasm we have opened up between *body* and *mind.* The conjunctive efforts of *and* are strained to a fare-thee-well, all but lapsing into body *or* mind. We ignore, if not deny, the intertwining inseparability of the two. We go to the Mayos in Minnesota for one, to the Menningers in Kansas for the other. We mindlessly exercise — one, two, one, two—or we body-scrunch in smoky chambers to analyze and study. Even now I am driving English wedges between the two. Let the Chinese word *hsin* speak for itself. A lovely splashing of energy makes the character that means either heart *or* mind. The choice—and the split—is in the translation.

My brush with the Chinese language did not restructure the architecture of my consciousness, but it has had its remodeling effects. I have begun to tear down the walls between opposites and live with them in a new way. In Chinese, opposites do not oppose each other so much as they define each other. They are not sent to live in mutual separation, but rather to share the same circle; poles apart, indeed, but interconnected. Even the word for opposite in Chinese demonstrates that relationship—it is *fan mien*, the *reverse face*.

The Chinese ask: What is the reverse face of small? Or at least the teachers of Chinese ask it. What is the reverse face of good? The reverse face of long? When you ask the length of something in Chinese you inquire after its long-short. When pricing something (language textbooks are always deep into commerce) you ask for its much-little.

Opposites in the Chinese language arise mutually and peaceably, as needful of one another as day needs night and as south needs north. There is not a war of ascendancy between them. They exist together synergistically.

The polarities in Chinese are represented by *yin/yang* and symbolized by the *t'ai chi t'u,* that circle with the S division that is black on one side, white on the other. In the black side is a small white dot, in the white side a small black dot. The black side is *yin*—the yielding, the dark, the feminine, the moon; the white side is *yang*—the forceful, the light, the masculine, the sun.

But do not understand this too quickly. The symbol is not meant to be rigidly fixed in equal halves, like fair shares of a Peter Paul Mounds. The curving center line represents the constancy of change, not the fixity of an equal division. Look at the curve as the ridged back of a dragon, half-hidden in the mist, moving now this way, now that. Now more *yin* makes up the circle, now more *yang*. The interplay is as constant as the changing way of the wind and the seasonal course of the river.

The symbol, then, does not mean simply that all opposites or polarities exist side by side. It means that they exist simultaneously in all things. It is not the *light* on this side and the *dark* on that, the *masculine* on this side, and the *feminine* on that, as a central aisle divides an auditorium. *Yin* is the yielding, the dark, the feminine in all things, in all of us, always. *Yang* is the forceful, the light, the masculine, in all things, in all of us, always.

Skiing is a perfect meditation on the *yin/yang*, an exercise in the understanding of it. The very thrust of the mountain depends on the hollowing spirit of the valley. Without one there would not be its other. Your skiing is a counterpoint of yielding and aggression—receiving the bumps and extending to fill the hollows. What could be more constant than the changeability, or more changeable than the constancy of snow and light and wind and sun?

Centered Skiing is an expression of the *yin/yang* in skiing, a union of the diverse, a balance of the extremes. Roberto Assagioli,

father of Psychosynthesis, spoke of "the power to play with opposites and establish a synthesis." Such is the way of Centered Skiing.

Some people feel threatened by the idea of synthesis. They see Centeredness as a stilling of passions, and a dulling of differences into a stolid mediocrity. The first season of the Centered Skiing workshops at Sugarbush, a skier from Montreal phoned me to ask about the program. He was interested in it, but he had some questions. I answered them, but I suspected he wasn't asking what he really wanted answered. After a second long conversation it came out. He was a strong, aggressive skier and he was afraid that being Centered might rob him of that.

The Montreal skier feared that Centeredness was a folding inward of extremes to make a bland pudding, a blending of *yin* and *yang* to come out gray. He feared Centeredness meant the giving up of some cherished part of himself, as if we might lobotomize or emasuclate him into some synthetic oddity. The fear of gray puddingness is not rare; I have encountered it often since, expressed and unexpressed.

Rest assured: What is abnormal is not the synthesis; it is the split, the One without its Other. Synthesis heals the split, but is not a compromise; harmony is not a limitation; balance is not a leveler. Look at the *t'ai chi t'u,* the *yin/yang* symbol on these pages. See the dragon's back carve the circle into two: the black and the white; separating and unifying at once. There is dependency, but the specific identity remains. It is not a circle of gray.

To understand that best, to appreciate it in your own totality, it is necessary to do something that is mending of opposites, joining of body and mind. Something that will demonstrate the One and its Other and their Unity to you directly. Something like *t'ai chi* or *aikido* or skiing with awareness.

THE SPLIT BRAIN

Being of two minds is not the simple metaphor it was once taken for. Recent studies indicate that the two hemispheres of the brain are not simply two halves of a whole, but are actually two distinct brains that have developed unique modes of organizing information. The two sides process the world and instruct the body in quite different ways.

It has long been known that the body is controlled in a criss-cross pattern by the brain's hemispheres—the left hemisphere controls the right side of the body, the right hemisphere controls the left. (The few exceptions are among left-handed people.) It has also been known that the verbal facility of the human animal is primarily a left-brained matter.

In the last part of the nineteenth century, scientists were busy mapping the dominant hemisphere, as they called it, pinning little claiming flags of specialty on the tiniest of territories—someone even claimed one small brain section as the seat of love-of-children. Other scientists objected to this overly-fine precision of location, but even those with more holistic views largely ignored the "minor" hemisphere as merely automatic in its functioning and subordinate to the verbal hemisphere.

That view has changed appreciably in recent decades. The bridge of nerve tissue called the *corpus callosum* that connects the brain's hemispheres is sometimes severed through injury or surgery. Recent research with such split-brained people, and with experimental animals, has focused attention on the long-belittled side of the brain that doesn't talk. The studies have found that there are equally important, albeit largely nonverbal, specialties on that side of the house, too. A partial list of the attributes of each side could look like this:

Left Hemisphere	Right Hemisphere
(Right side of the body)	(Left side of the body)
Sequential	Simultaneous
Logical	Intuitive
Analytical	Synthetical
Rational	Metaphorical
Digital	Analogic
Relational	Integrative
Linear	Spatial
Apollonian	Dionysian
Verbal	Imagery

The left-brained list has been most revered in our Western world. Being reasonable and logical are desirable attributes; being intuitive is a little spacy. There is foot-shifting in its presence. It is not asked to address the graduating class, and no doctorates are granted in its name. Words, too, are honored more than the silent play of images. A person who has a way with words gets further in this life—and even *getting further*, generally considered desirable, is a left-brained, linear notion of success.

In our wordy world, the very muteness of the right hemisphere has perhaps kept it from proper appreciation. Now, however, it is coming into its own. Imagery and intuition are gaining respectability. Einstein said his theory of relativity came to him in a visual image of a man riding on a ray of light. The chemist Kekulé got his insight into the structure of the benzene ring from a dream of a serpent with its tail in its mouth. Dreams seem to be right-brained matters.

The creative flashes of the right hemisphere are analyzed, shaped, and edited by the logical left brain, whose credit line has often loomed large on the final report. But now the silent member of the partnership is being recognized.*

Skiing is largely right brained. The body's orientation in space, the images of movement, all are the currency of the right hemisphere. Yet a cloud of words and left-brainedness surrounds the sport. Instructors explain and suggest, and books and magazines are gray with words of analysis and linear advice. However, merely cutting out the words is no guarantee that the instruction of skiing would be any more right-brained oriented. Indeed, wordless instruction is not necessarily more *nonverbal*. An instructor who teaches only by demonstration has no assurance that his

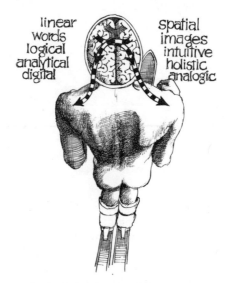

student is not prattling to himself subvocally, his left hemisphere busily spinning syntax and sentences about the silent parade before him.

Indeed, someone used to learning and living with words who is suddenly plunged unprepared into a nonverbal situation can suffer a kind of withdrawal symptom that could impede rather than further his learning. In teaching experiments with ski schools some students in the classes that were taught nonverbally interpreted the instructor's silence as indifference.

---

*For further reading on the brain and its hemispheres see the Booklist for works of Robert Ornstein, Julian Jaynes, Bob Samples and Ragnar Granit.

Words, then, are a symptom of the problem, not the problem itself. The problem is getting stuck in the inappropriate brain center, the one in which logic and analysis reign, while engaged in a right-brained activity. Simply cutting off the words does not change the orientation. Calling a bird a fish does not make it a swimmer.

Instructors who want to cut down on verbal explanation and teach more by demonstration would do well to prepare their students in advance by getting them in a right-brained mode. Paradoxically, they can *tell* them of their intention; that can help. They can also play games and do exercises to get their students in a right frame of brain, so to speak. At Sugarbush we use guided fantasy and exercises in visualization and imagery (see Chapter 7).

We have also done some chanting and meditation, which are possibly right-brain stimulants, but we haven't yet explored an area that holds some promise—*singing.* Yodeling while skiing might be more than a Swiss tourist attraction. It seems that the right hemisphere is not without verbal ability entirely (a certain referential capacity that leads to naming and categorizing is missing). The right side of the brain has words in song, for instance. Aphasics, people who have lost the power of understanding or using speech or written words through strokes or other lesions, can often still sing songs they previously knew. (Some can still swear, too). And words or phrases are sometimes appropriately responded to by split-brained people without their cognition of the word itself.

The right words, then, in the right form rather than no words at all are necessary to communicate with the right side of the brain, that side most involved with skiing. The directly triggering words, the image-forming words should be sought—anything that keeps the right-brained pictures from being scrambled by left-brained participles.

As you ski, attend to the images, not the words. Pull the plug on the digital processing machinery and tune into the analogic. Stay with the images; they are the thoughts of the right hemisphere. They are most appropriate to skiing. Learn to translate instructors' words into images and forebear converting images to words—hastening to put every experience into a jar and labeling it. Let that happen by itself; it will soon enough. Play the images before your eyes until the matching words roughen on your tongue by themselves. You will then have appropriate metaphors to call on again (see Chapter 9).

BALANCE

References in the everyday world to the right and left hemispheres of the brain have become common; there is almost a fad quality about it, as if here were a new game, such as what's *U* or *Non-U*, what's *in* or *out*, what's *upperbrow, middlebrow*, or *lowbrow*. Some divisionists have their flags out again to designate overly specific territories. And some people, who can't shake the habit of splitting the unsplittable, have welcomed the attention to the hemispheres of the brain as the New Dualism, more modern and more respectable that the body/mind division that recently held them in thrall.

What is of overriding importance in the matter of the brain's hemispheres is not the division between them but the unity—a synergy. The corpus callosum is a busy two-way bridge, not a Berlin wall. There is interchange and there is wholeness. The information on either side is equally important to the whole—like stereo speakers. *Balance* is the key. Bring the percussion down so as not to drown out the strings.

The brain's left side has enjoyed a long term of predominance over the right hemisphere. It is now the right hemisphere's turn—but not to dominate: that is not the issue. The issue is balance.

Along with the new attention to the silent hemisphere, will come a new way of expressing a total-brained *understanding* or *knowing*. Those two words are too tie-and-jacket left brained to serve the purpose of the whole. Needed is a physical word of imagery, such as *understand* once was (to stand under). I like *grok*, the word from *Stranger in a Strange Land*. It has that necessary quality of pervasive knowing and of liking as well; but there is nothing inherently physical in it. Another word has more going for it—it is common, it is short, and it implies movement. It is the word *dig*. When you are skiing under a winter-white sun, when your *ch'i* is written in perfect tracks on perfect snow, comes a total moment when you really, really understand, when you wholly know—in intellect, in feeling, in body, and in both brains. That's when you *dig* it.

4

Hang loose

GROOVING
WITH
GRAVITY

*I don't know who discovered water, but I'm
sure it wasn't a fish.* **— MARSHALL McLUHAN**

"Something there is that doesn't love a wall, that wants it down."
I'm reminded of Frost's words as I walk the wooded hills behind
my Vermont house. This is second growth on once cleared land,
now returned to wild, and I come across stone walls, lining straight
as shadows across rise and hollow, through the trees. Some walls
are a sprawl of rocks now, tossed by the seasonal heaving of the
ground, that slow leaf-molded ocean. But some are still standing
against frost and freshet through forgotten years. Clearly something there is that *loves* a wall, as well. It is gravity.

Gravity loves the wall and gravity wants it down. The walls
that stand do so by grace of the very same forces that have
tumbled the walls that no longer stand. The same pull that has
made a huggermugger pile of these stones keeps these a wall, one
stone atop the other supporting the other that supports another in

an integrated structure that rides out the sighs of the earth. Thus there exists in time the structure/process that is called a wall. These other stones, fallen, are a less-structured process called a heap. I've watched the same inexorable tug at work on old barns, too. The barns have stood against a century of heavy snows, slewing slightly through the years, perhaps—adjusting, shifting. Then one spring, they're down, a shapeless slump of timbers and curled shingles. Some critical agreement in the tenuous relationship of "I'll hold you up and you hold that up and I'll lean on that" has been broken. Gravity, which made it a barn, kept its roof on, and weighted its timbers in place, now brings it all down as the delicate balance fails.

Bodies live in the same gravity as barns and walls. All movement, all activity, from the blink of an eye to the leap of a Nureyev, is backgrounded by gravity. Gravity shapes us as water shapes a fish and few have experienced its release, except moon travelers and maybe those who float in John Lilly's darkened tank.

Gravity is certainly the skier's ocean. He sports in it like a dolphin. Even the most sedate downhilling skier depends on gravity for motive force. Racers scheme with gravity to favor their downhill path. Jumpers hollow their bodies to stretch longer arcs against its graph. And freestyle skiers play puppy games with it, yapping at its heels, seeking "air" in teasing spurts and creative patterns.

Skiers off skis live in gravity, too, and how they deal with it in their mundane bare-ground lives affects their ability to use it on the slope.

FIELDS WITHIN FIELDS

The body is a structure/process that can be balanced in gravity's field, interrelating and interacting in such a way that these bones, these bones seem to walk around as lightly as though mounted like a chandelier, as loose as a scribble, with dangling easy movements. Dancing. Gliding. Or a body can be out of whack with gravity, always fighting with it, shortening muscles into a rigid rebellion: the knees thrust back into a lock, the pelvis thrown into a tilt, and the head dropped forward on its stem fighting the pull.

Look upon the body (or better the body/mind because only in words can we separate the inseparable) as an energy field set within the larger energy field of gravity, the forces augmenting each other or canceling each other—cooperating or clashing. How well a person functions—mentally, physically, emotionally—

depends on how his personal field relates to the larger fields in which he lives; whether, in short, he is sustained by gravity (fed by it) or attacked by it.

The human form is anatomically a daring creation set in gravity's field with built-in instability. People are not constructed like stone walls or barns—or even like four-legged animals with supports at the corners; people are more like inverted pyramids, adventurously balanced. Unlike the grinning dolls that rock upright on rounded bottoms, the living body wears its center of gravity high, above a bifurcated lower section. Constant, though unnoticed, adjustments are needed to remain erect. Energy is needed to keep one of those dolls down; energy is needed to keep a real person up.

The human form sacrifices stolid stability for a dynamic relationship with its world. More subject to falls, more dependent on balance—inherently a risk-taker—the human body has earned a flexibility of directional movement unshared by other creatures. The human figure has, for instance, an ability to turn quickly around a central core: to rotate. This ability, in use, can be as dazzling as Dorothy Hamill's spin, or as ponderous as a waiter's change of direction when he sees you signaling over the soup. Four-legged beasts do not have this pivotal turning ability, which accounts in part for the humor (and pathos) inherent in a dog chasing its tail or a bear on hind legs dancing heavily to an accordion.

Gravity's force appears to act upon a body in a flagpole line, a narrow vertical set perpendicular to the earth's surface. This is the core, the stillpoint around which Dorothy Hamill spins, around which we all turn. How symmetrically a body seems to operate around that core determines how well the individual's field relates to gravity's field, how fully it sups at gravity's table. The relationship is a dynamic relationship, the body parts co-operating in space and in activity. "Posture" and all its implications of fixed and firm military rigidity have no place here. We are concerned with use and *balance in use.*

When the body parts are misaligned, balance is compromised and gravity is less friendly. The tussle is on. Such bodies seem to reject the agreement nature made; that is, accept the uncertainties inherent in the upright position and you will be graced with a marvelous facility for movement.

The bodies that say no to this are futilely seeking the impression of stability in their rigidity. They stump across the earth on insensitive legs and stand as locked as possible, pretending to a control that is illusory. Their shoulders hunch to the challenge, their heads jut forward. They are unyielding, hanging on. Even the jaws clench.

All such bodies have abdicated much of their right to freedom in movement; yet, they have not bought the stability they are paying for. On the contrary, their insistence on stability has made them even more unstable and has shorted their animal righting reflexes with an overriding tension. Such bodies are more easily upended by a patch of ice or a loose rug on a waxed floor. Such minds—inseperable from the physical attitude—are more easily upended, too, on the metaphorical ice patches and loose rugs along life's path.

How often have you, as a skier, tensed against a possible fall only, thus, to guarantee it? To ski into a sea of moguls with a fixed knee and a fixed notion is the surest way to project yourself into the timber. Only when the body is allowed to function as it was meant to—with the least interference from inappropriate brain centers—can the knees compress and extend in direct response to the sensing of the bumps, not in response to some sluggish thought about "absorption." If the body is allowed its freedom in gravity—and it can be unshackled from confining habits with some conscious attention and learning-to-allow—it will move better, ski better.

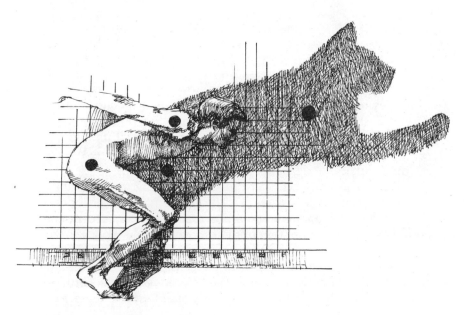

There are other forces, besides gravity, to which we have inured our awareness and habituated ourselves to ignore-ance. For instance, the tilt and the turn of the earth bringing cycles of light and tide and seasons. We direct little conscious attention to these forces. But gravity is the most directly affecting. Most of the stimuli that arrive for processing by our nervous system are from muscular activity triggered by gravity. In short our front office spends most of its time dealing with routine requests to keep us from collapsing, to keep the head off the chest, the body off the floor. No matter how properly our bones are balanced one above the other, like a stack of chairs in a juggler's act, the muscles are constantly making little adjustments—shortening or being lengthened against their antagonists—to keep the whole shebang from clattering into a pile. Some people's muscles do a better job than others. More efficiently, more economically, more simply, more aesthetically. Just as some skiers ski with more finesse, more lightly, more pleasingly.

THE DIFFERENT TWITCHES

Muscles that move the bones about do so by shortening (contracting). They do that in opposition to their counterparts or antagonists—one pulling with the other relaxing, one flexing with the other extending. These are skeletal muscles, sometimes called voluntary muscles because they appear to be more readily controllable by conscious volition than the so-called involuntary muscles of the heart and the viscera. The skeletal muscles are striped, made up of what could be likened to handfuls of tiny wires in a telephone cable. And like telephone wires they are color-coded—a reddish fiber and a pale one. The red ones contract more slowly and fatigue more slowly than the pale ones. The pale ones contract quickly and fatigue relatively quickly. All skeletal muscles appear to be a mixture of these two fibers in varying proportion. The fibers are also graphically characterized as "slow twitch" (red) and "fast twitch" (pale).*

---

*Dr. David Costill of the Ball State University Human Performance Laboratory has tested world-class runners—long distance and sprint specialists—in an effort to determine whether there is any correlation between the predominance of one sort of fiber or the other in the runners' muscles and their preference for long or short distances. There appears to be. Short twitchers are the sprinters, long twitchers the long distance runners. Which came first, the twitch or the speciality has not yet been determined.

The skeletal muscles get the message to move from the motor nerves, part of an intricate network involving switching systems using chemical and electrical connections and directed by control centers in the brain and spinal cord. It is all intricately complex and fascinating, and this summary is the same as saying telephones are tin cans connected by wires. But there is, one hopes, enough truth in it to be of value.

THESE BONES

Now consider the skeleton. Mentally hang the skeleton from a point in the top of its skull, a point which would mark an extension of its spine. Suspended from that crown point, the bones hang loosely; the feet tread the floor lightly, but firmly. All is in order.

Bones dressed with flesh and the full complement of muscles, tendons, et al., can appear to hang in that same loose fashion. Indeed, a person organized around a still central core whose body sections are stacked neatly, but not rigidly, one on top of the other will have that easy look. A body that has a full sense of its skeleton seems to move with an ease and lightness that is usually called grace, a warmer word for efficient.

We would all appear more graceful (more economical in our use of muscles and energy) if, for instance, we rose from seating as if sky-hooked to our feet from that hanging point in the spine-top of our skull. If we could lie on the floor as flat as our undressed bones would allow, we would know that there were no unnecessary muscle contractions arching the small of our backs or keeping other points of the body aloft. A reclining body, *completely* relaxed, is like that skeleton—though padded, it is unimpeded from being as flat as possible.

See if you can lie like a bag of bones on the floor. Practice moving about as if you were nothing but your bones, a dancer in the *danse macabre*. Discover something from your skeletal self about your habitual tensions.

Lie easy. Sit easy—a puppet skeleton just a-jangle with easy.*

Alas, it is not always that easy. We have been too long in our bodies not to have brought about some far (and deep) reaching modifications in their structures, and thus in their functions. (And in their functions and thus in their structures—one is the other.) In short, our lives are showing.

Muscles living in the persistent contraction of tension have lost the memory of ease. Muscles long overstretched, like a spring

---

*Leroy R. "Satchel" Paige, arguably the best pitcher of baseballs in the game's history, has some notions about living young, one of which is, "Keep the juices flowing by jangling around gently as you move."

on a screen door constantly banging in the wind, have lost the resiliency to snap back. Then, instead of our bodies expressing an emotion as "a single response to an immediate situation" (Dr. Ida Rolf's words), they are locked into a pattern which may or may not be appropriate to the moment. Such a body is a broken record stuck in one groove of expression. Such a person, Dr. Rolf says, "...henceforth...lives, moves and has his being in an attitude."

Freeing this being from his frozen attitude, changing habitual body uses for something more simple, and efficient, usually takes more than the warm, bright light of awareness. It takes time, attention, and knowledgeable work, and it proceeds best with outside expert help.*

GROUNDING

The apparent lightness of the well-aligned body is not a flimsy, wafted-about lightness. There is, with the upward thrust, a flowing downward as well. Indeed, some people, experiencing for the first time their personal energy field in harmonious relationship with the gravitational field, describe the sensation as "heavier." What they are sensing is the downward course of their *ch'i*. What they are experiencing is groundedness, contact, connectedness. Maybe they have been flighty types—birds, hard put to alight. Or they might be those who have deadened their legs with tension, holding their energy high in their chest—breathing there exclusively—and holding on to the world hard with their eyes.

When they experience the dissipation of their customary background tension and a letting-go of the holding-on in their thighs, they open a conduit for energy in their legs. The unfamiliar downrush of sensation is experienced as heaviness; not as a ponderous weight, however, but rather as a putting down of roots—a connection from which sustenance can be drawn.

Not strangely, really, lightness and heaviness are *both* correct responses to a coming to the core, an awareness of Center. What has been touched is balance, the stillpoint. What is being experienced is Centeredness; a body/mind in relaxed readiness. Connected to the universal energy, fed by it, *ch'i* flows freely. Circles within circles, unending. No irrelevant muscle contractions impede the *ch'i*, no crimping tensions divert it, no abruptly

---

*A list of some "body/mind shops," a brief description of various techniques, and addresses of some institutes and organizations specializing in the various procedures are in the Appendix.

angular breaks slow its current. All is at ease, alive, alert.

In this way of being in the world the breath is full and unforced. It comes and goes as simply, as surely, as the tides. The feet make a sure, equal contact with the ground—not planted like fence posts are planted, but planted like fruit trees are planted. Alive, the feet are free to feel the pulses of the earth, and do.

Movement starts at the body's core, in the pelvic region and flows outward to be refined, defined, particularized by the periphery—by the arms, hands, legs, feet. Inner to outer. Beginning in what Koichi Tohei calls the singlepointinthelowerabdomen, *seika-no-itten*. Here is the *hara,* the *kath,* the *tan t'ien.*

Field of Cinnabar.
Solar plexus.
The Center.

This, then, is how it is to be in harmony with the fields of forces—internal, external—to be jangling along grooving with gravity.

Such is the relaxed/alert position familiar to martial artists, a body/mind receptive to any *possible* change, but not tensed by the expectation of any *particular* change. A body capable of moving with alacrity in any direction without the need for preliminary adjustments. There is no need to shift weight in preparation, no need for "getting" the body ready to move. It *is* ready, now, poised at Point Zero without bias: a body/mind relaxed/alert, capable of moving with the most effect for the least effort.

Such is, as well, the General Position on skis: relaxed/alert, expecting nothing, ready for anything. No tension knots block the energy flow. The breathing is easy, the neck and head loose.

The upper body is erect, not jack-knifed. It is stilled, but not *held* still. Still the way a pine tree in a windless evening is still.

The shoulders are given easily to gravity, not held hunched to the ears. The arms lie in an open curve, embracing the energy radiating from the Center. The poles are held with a firm ease so that the tips can be touched to the ground with a simple flexion of the wrist—touched lightly, precisely, as if making an electrical connection.

The knees are easy—not *bent*, but *bending*.

The feet are not dead in the boots, casketed in fiberglass, and plastic. They are alive, open conduits for the flow of *ch'i* which they direct along the skis, seemingly pressing it, extruding it, against the snow. The bottom of the skis, the honed edge, is the line of contact between the physical manifestation of *your energy field* and the physical manifestation of *gravity's field*. It is the interface of exterior and interior, of the You and the Not-you. Two things that are the One. Ten thousand things and Unity.

Be conscious of those edges, of those forces. Relish them. Ride them with delicacy and reverence.

5

SON OF
GROOVING
WITH
GRAVITY

Ever wonder why someone doesn't try softer?
— LILY TOMLIN

There is a way of using the body that is perfectly suited to the task at hand. A *basal effort* that is just enough to get the job done with the least wear and tear. It might be called the Baby Bear Effort. Not too soft, not too hard. In the words of Goldilocks, "just right." Whatever the job—toting barges, lifting bales, or quietly sitting in a chair and sipping tea—there is an optimal expenditure of energy, a particular marshaling of musculature that is totally relevant to the task. Ideally there is in the action nothing superfluous, nothing redundant, nothing contradictory.

Bodies used so aptly are aesthetically stirring to watch whether they belong to dancers, athletes, or construction workers. Such bodies are also rare. Our culture appears to be overpopulated with Papa Bears, splattering the landscape with the excesses of the old college try—straining, overdoing, grimacing at jar lids. And you need only glance at a ski hill to see evidence of overdoing there, most of it not only wasteful but counter-productive. Habits of excess have made us adept at doing a thing and its opposite at the same time. We spend much of our lives doing the bodily equivalent of stepping on the brakes and the accelerator simultaneously.

I ask the workshop skiers to make hooks of their hands by bending their fingers; then I tell them to interlock left hand with right and try to pull them apart. Much strain and effort, of course. "Why not this?" I simply straighten my fingers and the hands separate. Groans. You didn't say we could do that!

Nor did I say you couldn't.

The exercise is simply an illustration of our readiness to accept an adversary relationship within ourselves, an interior warring in which a Goodie Shouldie battles a plaintive I Can't. We ignore the simpler choices that require no increase in effort. We trundle in ever bigger guns to overwhelm the opposition, and yet, in the words of Walt Kelly's Pogo, "We has met the enemy and they is us."

In order to *force* yourself to do something there must be a *resistance* to overcome. (You cannot force yourself to bend your knees unless you are resisting bending your knees.) Instead of piling force on force, how much simpler it is to *let go* of the resistance. Flatten your fingers and let go. The force is yours. The resistance is yours. The choice is yours.

MOVERS AND FAKERS

The *basal effort* needed in any situation has also been called *optimal tonus** because there is just enough muscle contraction (tonus) for the task, and no more. To see optimal tonus in operation watch a cat jump on a table. Hathaway, my calico, approaches the table where I sit working. Crouching slightly, her lion-colored eyes fix the table's edge. Such a totality of attention! I wonder what's happening in that furry skull—what chemical and electrical connections are measuring and sending messages. Comes the tiniest suggestion of contraction; release, and she is on the table, flowing over the rim to alight at the very crest of her upward arc. There is not enough excess in her movement to stir one sheet of paper. (The smug sweep of her tail takes care of that.)

---

*Bernard Gunther, *Sense Relaxation: Below Your Mind.*

Some athletes are cat-like in their economy of movement. Julius Erving, of the Philadelphia 76ers, comes immediately to mind. Dr. J. is so purely in cahoots with gravity he can apparently neutralize it at will. Then there is O.J. Simpson with a football.

These smooth movers and fakers are known as *naturals* and are held in awe; but somehow they are not as universally cherished as that other athletic extreme—the excessive tryer who succeeds! Because, make no mistake, though effort may be counter-productive, the production of it can be so awesome that there *is* no counter. Witness Pete Rose, of Cincinnati, for instance, winner of a number of Most Valuable awards and the Hickock belt, emblematic, as they say in the sports pages, of his athletic accomplishments. Pete Rose is a singularly successful ballplayer, although economy is not his forte. He is master of excess. He kills snakes at third and explodes in busting efforts around the bases. We call it "hustle" and cheer it lovingly. Little League coaches urge their young players to emulate him. Try! Try! Try!

In the 1975 World Series there was another ballplayer, also a Most Valuable. Watch Fred Lynn's easy strides consume the fields of Fenway—*optimal tonus* personified. There is nothing irrelevant in his movement, nothing excessive in it to be lumped as hustle. His is the kind of movement you notice more in the having moved.

Not many coaches hold up naturals as a model to the youngsters in their charge. The prevailing opinion is that you are either a natural or you are not. And if you are not? Then, they say, make up for it by *trying.* Everyone can try, if they try. True, trying hard has enough apparent success to be much favored and honored. Its negative sides are unknown or unnoticed. We live by the Philosophy of Overwhelm. (See Chapter 10.)

Actually the gift of fluid movement and appropriate effort is one granted all but a few; but it is a gift generally compromised, squandered, and misplaced over the years. As we grow day by day, we make our deals with gravity and collect our share of frustrations—dangling in awkward steps from the fingers of encouraging adults, falling off garage roofs, hunching over homework, cringing from real or imagined physical and psychic blows; in short, by our habitual responses and attitudes, we give ourselves our shapes. And our shapes, in turn, shape our further responses and attitudes. Thus is the high gloss of our sensory abilities grimed over and dulled with disuse. Instead of stripping our gifts back to their shining basics, we slap on another thick coat of effort.

HOME

Every body, every mind has a *home,* a base which feels right because it is familiar—never mind the stresses and muscular excesses that are objectively present. For some, their so-called relaxed state is extreme muscular contraction. Excess is the norm for them; they are used to it. It is *home.* Not only are the necessary antigravity muscles at work; not only is the Baby Bear Effort needed to raise the teacup in operation, but in use as well is an entire army of contractions that is never at ease. Such people might be so tight that they twang, but for them that is "relaxed." It is *home.*

The most extreme states of tension can be accepted as standard if they are familiar. Jack Downing, who is a medical doctor, a head doctor, and a rolfer among other things, told me about a woman who came to him complaining of severe headaches. She thought she might be too tense. "Yes, you are tense," he agreed, "This muscle feels like a bone." Surprise: "You mean it isn't?"

Awareness of excessive muscle tension can be helpful in letting it go. Sometimes the very flood of that awareness is enough to break the dam, but not always, not for everyone. Holding on to the holding-on is common. There is something essentially conservative in us that resists change—even change for the better. Be it ever so uptight, *home* is *home!*

Being relaxed, then, is not necessarily a pleasant state, particularly for someone thrust suddenly—a stranger in a strange land—into the unaccustomed calm of tension-free space. There must be a readiness for it—physically, emotionally, mentally—if the new pact with gravity is going to be met with relief and joy rather than consternation and allowed to last. Some body-work techniques can almost miraculously usher people into that world of minimized tension, but how long they choose to remain depends to a great extent on their readiness to live in the new easy way—their willingness to leave *home* for the unfamiliarity of a new one.

A friend studying to be an Alexander Technique teacher told me about a visitor to her class, who agreed to be a subject for demonstration. The seemingly magical hand-on-the-neck—the stock in trade of the expert Alexander practitioner—produced in him an obvious and sudden relaxation of his neck and shoulders. (The neck muscles are deemed the body's *primary control* in Alexander's theory as we shall see below.) By now, accustomed to the reluctance with which people yield their miseries, the class members kept a sidelong eye on their visitor. "As we went on to other things," my friend said, "we watched him moving his neck about with a puzzled expression. He was probably wondering where his familiar tension had gone. He finally found it. He seemed terribly relieved that he didn't have to be relaxed any more." She smiled. "If nothing else, I've learned this year how comforting our discomforts are to us!"

The same thing happens in skiing. Instructors have long been puzzled by the tenacity with which pupils hang on to faults, the very faults they have bought a ski school ticket to have corrected. Even though apparently pleased with the day's progress, they hasten to re-embrace their errant ways. They have not yet chosen to let go of their resistance, to really leave *home*. They are just visiting.

In teaching, if instructors try to wrest their students' habits from them they will meet with as little success as they would if they snatched a security blanket from a child. Nothing lasting has been achieved. Bad skiing habits are only the more obvious part of a system of actions, a totality of responses, and the relationships within that system are what need readjustment if any changes are to "take." It is the task of instructors to use their expertise to look at the whole, to spot just how their pupils have snarled the yarn, where it leads from there, and direct the pupils' awareness to the key knots. The snarl then becomes a puzzle that the two, instructor and pupil, are working on *together*—with deep interest, but without judgment or an undercurrent of unconscious competition. ("Give me that fault!" "Just try and take it!")

"Before I started teaching in the Centered Skiing workshops," Martin said, "I was exhausted after a lesson. I felt I'd been battling with my students, trying to *force* them to learn something from me. It was infuriating when I'd see them the next day back to their old habits. Now we seem to learn *together*. If they want to hang on to some fault now, it's fine with me; but it seems the faults fall away more easily when they stop feeling they have to fight me over them."

No one takes kindly to being evicted, however unsuitable *home* may be.

F.M. ALEXANDER AND SELF

F. Mathais Alexander was an Australian whose notion it was that there are certain ways of using the body (he called it *self*) that are better than others. He believed that most of the civilized world had settled dully into the less than better ways—hanging on to habits that were wrong (inefficient), but *felt right* because people were used to them. As a result, man suffered. Maybe aches, maybe angst. But most certainly he suffered the failure of living to his full capacity—physically, emotionally, and mentally.

Alexander had suffered from a disability devastating to a professional elocutionist which he was—periodic loss of his voice. After the traditional methods failed to rid him of these visitations, he set out, with little more than a mirror and prodigious self-discipline, on a long trail of discovery. He found that the fault was in the way he used his *self,* the habitual responses involved with what he called *end-gaining* instead of the *means whereby* through which that end was gained. In short, he was playing for results instead of attending to the process.

His principle reached far beyond the use of the voice, although he cured many confirmed stutterers. All movement became his study. He taught his principle in Britain and the United States until his death in 1955 and gained a famous following, including Aldous Huxley, George Bernard Shaw, and John Dewey. At one time it was the peak of chic to "go to Alexander." His technique has survived fashionableness and is now enjoying a deserved renaissance. Its applications to skiing are particularly apt.*

The Alexander theory of *primary control,* mentioned earlier, holds that any tension in any part of the body is reflected in the head and neck muscles. Any deviation from optimal tonus, any compensations in the musculature anywhere, is registered in the muscles that extend and flex the head, specifically in the *upper trapezius* (the higher reaches of that muscle which fans like a manta ray across the upper back), and in the *sternocleidomastoid* muscles (the cord-like muscles that lead from behind the ears to the chest). It works the other way, too. Any excessive tension in the head and neck muscles resonates throughout the trunk and legs, according to his theory.

Any Alexander teacher worthy of the name can read the secrets of a subject's uses and abuses of his body by merely placing a light hand on the nape of the neck. It is said that when Alexander put his hand on a certain pupil's neck he asked, "And how did you injure your left knee, Dr. Feldenkrais?" Moshe Feldenkrais had a "soccer knee," all right, and he studied with Alexander, drawing on many Alexandrian insights on his way to evolving his own unique approach to the body and its behavior, but it seems that the story has gained a little in frequent telling. "He asked me if I ever had injured my knee," Dr. Feldenkrais said, when I played reporter and sought the facts.

To a skier, the neck muscles are of particular importance because of their bearing on balance. The carriage of the head has a major influence on a turn, but maybe not, as generally believed, because of the *weight* of the head. Rather, it could be because of a *special relationship* between the head and neck muscles and the muscles of the trunk and legs.

The Alexandrians hold that there are *reflexive responses* by muscles in the trunk and legs triggered by certain attitudes of the head. This notion marked an original application to human beings of responses long studied in animals, an application which impressed the eminent biologist, George E. Coghill, the first "hard" scientist to acknowledge favorably this innovative layman's discovery.

---

*See Appendix for addresses to reach Alexander teachers.

In animals there is something called the *righting reflex*. It's what makes a cat land on its feet when dropped bellyside up. Notice (if you have an affable cat handy) that it is the animal's head that leads the twist to proper alignment with the world; the rest of the body follows. Look fast; it happens in a blur.

There is that same subcortical, automatic righting reflex in the human animal, too. Within you, in short, is an automatic aid to balance—to recovery from imbalance. But it is automatic only if it is allowed to function freely. It can be short-circuited by upper-brain interference, or by habitual misuse of the body. Your balancing mechanism can be jammed by excessive tension in the neck, and put—I prefer to call it—on *manual override,* eliminating its appropriate automatic aspects.

Classically, drunks and small children right themselves, undamaged, from tumbles that could shatter the sober adult. Maybe it is that they are on *automatic*—either too out of it or too into it to tense themselves inappropriately into *manual override.* They are operating on the level of their animal righting reflex.

It's likely we've all had some experience of a miraculous recovery, on skis or off, that left us with a "now-who-did-that?" astonishment. Centered, harmoniously balanced, we can respond automatically to the forces of the greater field of energy in which we live. Tuned into these forces—whether by happenstance or by conscious training in Centering techniques—we flow with the universal flow. Our bodies are allowed to function as they were designed to function in such circumstances—*reflexively* without interference from inappropriate neocortical centers.

Besides being tied into the righting reflex, it seems our neck muscles are also related to certain other reflexive responses in the legs in such a way that, when unimpeded by irrelevant tensions, the act of standing up, for instance, is made remarkably less effortful. Thus our bodies are capable of working *with* gravity while standing up *against* gravity. It seems to be all in the original plans, but lost through carelessness and excess.

Standing up is one of the simple tasks we do every day that is the most larded with excessive effort. There is so much gathering of force, so much "getting set" with the entire body one might think we are off to the Augean stables. Thigh muscles tighten needlessly. Maybe even the jaw sets. And most assuredly the chest muscles grab enough to stop the breath. It is hardly noticeable, but there is a little—moment—there where the breath is held.

Notice it now. Find a straight chair and see what you do when you get up and down. Don't try to "do it right" or change anything, just do it and observe carefully what you actually do getting up from a chair. Place your palms on your thigh muscles. Do they tighten while you are still seated, "getting ready" ro rise? Do you push against the floor with your feet even before they bear any standing weight? When rising, do you lead with your chin, swooping it down and forward to gain momentum?

A jutting chin is a sure sign that the critical muscles at the back of your neck have been *shortened,* the most common misuse of those key muscles. According to the Alexander theory, the tension in those neck muscles is related to the other excessive tensions in the body. It is that tension-in-the-neck that overrides the reflexive response in the legs that would otherwise willingly assist in bringing you to standing. The Alexandrians say we have erased a built-in assist mechanism by shortening the neck muscles (jutting out the chin), and therefore need more effort to raise the body against gravity. If we, instead, allowed the neck muscles to ease and allowed the spine to lengthen through that sky-hook point in the skull, we would be plugging into the *reflexive response* in the legs and rise to our feet with greater ease.

In the skiing workshops we use a particular gimmick to show us whether or not our neck muscles are tight, our chest constricted, and our head held rigidly. I call it the "O.J. Move." It is named for O.J. Simpson, and is inspired not by his juke moves on charging linemen, but by his "Superstar in Rent-a-Car" TV commercials. Ever notice how he keeps his head in a constant mini-bopping motion, like one of those Mandarin dolls you see on car ledges? That is the O.J. Move. It reminds the neck and head to stay easy. And, if we can't keep that little motion going, it indicates to us we have clamped those critical muscles into rigidity. Rigidity in the neck means that the breath has caught too. The O.J. Move works on the slope, as well, easing us past those small breath-pausing moments, such as turning into the fall line. If you can keep the O.J. Move going—that tiny motion of your head, so small as to be almost invisible—it helps keep the breath flowing. Loose as Juice. That's the way to ski.

RELAX IS NOT THE WORD

There is excess in the way we lead our lives. We are told that we must relax. For many, relaxing means taking their tension on holiday. A mere change of venue—from the office to the tennis court, the mountains or the golf course. Our determination to get it right goes along. In our society it is even worth points to be known as someone who "can't relax." (Works hard, plays hard—promote that person!) For all its discussed dangers, stress is still the best address in this world that we have built.

"Relax!" an instructor advises a rigid skier. The skier, frozen from a combination of cold, fear of falling, and eagerness to please—or at least not look like a klutz—and habitually insensitive to the messages from his proprioceptors anyway, smiles wanly and tries another turn with knees fixed as rigidly as a lug wrench and with poles gripped in a gloved vise. Surely to yield one smidgen of that control would mean instant loss of it all. A catastrophe. So hang on.

"Relax!" the tennis pro calls and the student's racket head obediently droops. That's not it either.

"Relax!" the golf pro tells his pupil. But then there is no life in the legs, no power in the swing, no *tschunk* to the hit. The golf swing *depends* on tension—a specific orchestration of it, methodically acquired and sequentially released. How can you relax and be tense, too?

We are caught in a whiplash of either/or opposites that simply do not apply. Attention is *at-tension;* relaxed is *blah.* (Robert McKim, in his wonderful book *Experiences in Visual Thinking,* refers to the extremes as the "aha" and the "ho-hum.") But there need be no opposition between "attention" and "relaxed." The two are states that can be mutually enhancing. Look again at a cat, sitting there, playing Egyptian statue. Quiet. The motor barely ticks over. The muscles are soft and pliable. But *ready!* Such, too, is the way of the martial artist. Aha/ho-hum, relaxed/alert. Ready.

"Lax—showing little concern; remiss; negligent," the dictionary reads. And *re-,* of course, means to do it again. Do these sports professionals really want us to return to a state of *negligence* and *little concern?* No. Relax is the wrong word. It might even be the wrong concept. And binding it awkwardly with another word—relaxed/alert—as I have done in this book isn't the best answer either. (Somehow I cannot see ski instructors calling out, "Relax/alert, Agnes!" across the slopes.)

A better word might be "optimize!"—thus bringing forth from each and all the optimal muscle tonus for the task at hand, whether that task be a hook shot, a slap shot, or a shot-put.

There is another word for which I have higher hopes—
differentiate. Differential Relaxation is a term used by Edmund
Jacobsen, who also gave us Progressive Relaxation, a technique
now in use by many teams and individuals in sports.* Progressive
Relaxation involves the methodical focusing of attention on major
muscle groups in a particular order, tensing them, and then relaxing them. Although Jacobsen, when he presented his technique
in 1938, suggested some 200 training sessions, few practitioners
adhere to that regimen. Many people find variations of the technique, self-discovered, of value in relaxing.

Differential Relaxation involves becoming aware of the
differences between what Jacobsen calls *primary tensions* and
secondary tensions; that is, between those tensions (muscle contractions) that are necessary to do something, and those tensions
that are not necessary for the action but accompany it. Differential
Relaxation could just as well be called "differential contraction."
For every action the contraction of specific muscles is necessary,
but habitual misuse usually throws in dozens more that are unnecessary. That is wasteful. It is like turning on every light in the
house to read a postcard.

Check yourself now. What muscles do you *need* to hold
this book? To maintain your slump? Notice particularly any excessive tension in your shoulders. Are you a frowner? Touch that
spot between your eyes with your fingers and see for sure. As you
scan your body, *differentiate* between the muscles you need and
the muscles you can do without; and do without.

Ben Hogan narrowed the needs of the golf swing down to
the "inside" muscles—those that run along the insides of the calves
and thighs and the arms, differentiating those essential muscles
from the unessential ones along the outside of the body. (Later,
he further refined his differentiation and lessened the required
tension in the arms.)

Check yourself next time you are about to push off on
skis, or hit a golf shot, or serve a tennis ball. Scan your body
with awareness and observe your tensions. Have you turned on
more lights than you absolutely need? *Differentiate.* Turn off those
tensions that are unessential to the task at hand.

---

*Edmund Jacobsen, *You Must Relax*, McGraw-Hill, New York. Also look
for a Dell paperback called *RELAX: How You Can Feel Better, Reduce
Stress and Overcome Tension* edited by John White and James Fadiman.
It is a compendium of almost every known technique for relaxation.
The bibliography alone is worth the price of the book.

In a workshop on running directed by Mike Spino, author of *Beyond Jogging,* he had us progressively cut back our efforts. On a scale of 10, we reduced our effort from 9, to 8, 7, 6. Our speed, perversely, increased. Now less strained for, it came more easily, seemingly growing out of the ground and carrying us. In cutting down on the superfluous effort, we had reduced the redundant and contradictory muscle contractions. Our total effort was less, but the resulting vector was stronger and longer in the desired direction. We had tuned out the dissonances of our muscular misuse and were left with the quiet harmonics that meant our effort was a closer match to the task.

Al Chung-liang Huang, with whom I study *t'ai chi,* was trained in the exacting tradition of the classic Chinese theater and can differentiate the tiniest muscles in his face, thus giving him access to the infinite nuance of expression so important to that theater tradition. The differences are so small as to be almost subliminal.

Through conscious attention (benign and curious, not critical and demanding) to how you *actually* do things—not to how you *think* you do things or how you *ought* to do them—you can sharpen your ability to differentiate. Once freed of the tensions of goal-specific efforts your body will—happy surprise—seek a simpler means of doing on its own. No longer a Johnny-One-Note, the range in variation in muscle tonus will increase, and your ability to match the precise needs of the moment with the effort expended will be enhanced. Your physical responses will be more appropriate. You will, in effect, have replaced your old on-off switch (aha or ho-hum) with a finely differentiated rheostat. Happily, your new device has a marvelous capacity for automatic use, too.

Feldenkrais also uses the term *differentiate,* and as usual gets directly to the point. Differentiation is for him simply, "The sensing of differences and selecting the good over the useless." The good is the most efficient and economical.

In learning a motor skill, whether it be skiing or macrame, it is important to determine early which are the "good" tensions (relevant to the task) and which are the "useless." It is important because you will be practicing your new skill, and practice makes perfect only what you *are* practicing, not what you *think* you are practicing. If you do not *differentiate,* accentuating the positive and eliminating the unnecessary, you are forcing a fusion of the good and bad into an ever-tighter bond. Then separating the useless tensions from the useful ones will become more difficult. They will come in a set. With B you get egg roll—like it or not.

With your amalgam of moves, the useful with the useless, you are playing a switch version of Russian roulette. In this version the idea is to be sure-fire, and you have many empty chambers. You never know when a useless move will turn up—shanking the golf shot, netting your tennis ball, or skidding you out of a carved ski turn. You might come up with perfect shots and perfect turns— enough wrong things combining in the right way. You might have a whole series of good turns, a whole day's worth, or you might be hot on the tennis courts or the driving range. But with a technique burdened with nonessentials, you can as easily turn up a similar run of duds.

Repeatability suffers in relation to the number of irrelevancies in every action. Or as Ben Hogan put the same idea, "You cannot groove your compensations." Therefore, while you are learning, learn to *differentiate* from the start.

When I was learning to fly a few years ago, I found myself tending to adjust the trim tabs so that the airplane flew slightly nose heavy. Thus trimmed it made a discernible pressure on my left fingers where I held the yoke, or control wheel. The pressure was comforting to me because it was *definite* and the air seemed a remarkably indefinite place at the time. Only a few hours onward toward my license, however, I realized I had the makings of a bad habit. What I was doing in trimming the plane that way was creating a gross "feel" simply because I lacked the experience to detect a finer one. A foolish thing to do. If I wasn't *used* to anything yet, why get used to an overstatement when I could train myself in the same time to get used to a neutral state, a more desirable one for sensitivity to the airplane? With more time in the log book and careful attention to what was going on between me and One-Niner-Seven-Two-Tango we reached a mutual understanding, a stillpoint, a Center. The plane no longer had to lean on me for me to know it was there.

Delighted to have cut off a bad habit at the roots I mentioned the matter to Jack Murphy, general manager of Sugarbush and an experienced pilot. He laughed. Apparently such habits were common. "I knew a guy once always built in a crosswind," he said. That meant that the pilot was, in effect, turning both right and left at the same time. That was *home* for him. The result was a straight-ahead path, but with a greatly diminished margin of control. Whatever may be the opposite of differentiation, that's an example of it.

Like the pilot with his ersatz crosswind, some skiers build in similar undifferentiated excesses. Actually, many of the excesses practiced on the slopes today many of us paid good money to learn yesterday. The roundhouse of the old Arlberg-style rotation is a museum piece now, but there are many examples on the slopes of those who still cling to the more recent exaggerated reverse shoulder, or "comma" position, as *Sports Illustrated* dubbed it when it was new and seemed the ultimate.

By far the most common excess practiced on today's hills is one still widely taught—the up-and-down, rise-and-fall that sandwiches each turn. Traverse-rise-sink; traverse-rise-sink. It is a pleasant enough rhythm, and displeasing only to an eye not yet spoiled by the fine stillness at the core of the carved turn (see Chapter 11.) The up and down move is unnecessary for the un-weighting of the modern ski and, too—like the built-in crosswind—it limits control. The *up* breaks the steady pressure of the skis against the snow, and instead of the skis tracking around the arc of the turn as if on rails, they skid a wide wake on the snow—like a small sailboat without its centerboard down. Skidding is to deny the design of the modern ski the full flower of its art. The side camber of the ski is carefully calculated to cause it to carve an arc—if the skier will just *allow* it to happen.

The skidded turn is perfectly suitable on simple terrain where precision is unimportant, but if accuracy is a factor, or precise control desireable, the up-and-down movement becomes not only superfluous, but contradictory.

What's more if you have good honed-edged skis and proper boots, skidding your turns is denying them their natural expression— carving. It's like limiting a Ferrari to a supermarket parking lot.

Differentiation has a law that goes with it—the Weber-Fechner law: "The difference in stimulus that produces the least detectable difference in sensation is always in the same ratio to the whole stimulus."

It means that the smaller the weight you are holding, the smaller the portion of any change in weight—added or sub-tracted—you will be able to detect. For instance, if you (blind-folded) were holding a 20-pound chocolate cake and a fly landed on it, you would not be able to distinguish a difference; but if someone eased on a half pound of ice cream, you would—given an adequate nervous system—detect the difference. On a single piece of cake, a mere dollop of vanilla would register. And if the piece got small enough, you might notice the return of that fly.

What has this got to do with skiing? Well, Feldenkrais relates the Weber-Fechner law to the kinesthetic sense. "The smaller the exertion, the finer the increment or decrement that we can distinguish," he says. If you are tugging at a stuck drawer with optimal tonus, you notice the instant the stuck-ness changes— and you don't spread the contents of the drawer all over the floor. The smaller the exertion, the finer the differentiation of response in our muscles, and the closer we can come to matching the effort to the task.

"The lighter the effort we make," Feldenkrais says, "the faster is our learning of any skill, and the level of perfection we can attain goes hand in hand with the finesse we obtain." The more optimal the tonus (the more precise the differentiation) the easier it is to learn, and the more precise is the learning. So whatever you are doing, do less of it. Turn out those lights.

Some athletes, already blessed with finesse, delight in refining their differentiation into spun threads. Sigi Grottendorfer, Director of the Sugarbush Ski School, is such a one. He carves away at his carved turns, whittling them ever finer just as some craftsman from his native Austria might carve wood. Simplify, simplify. I call him the Thoreau of ski instructors. "If I didn't think there was always something to discover, I wouldn't ski any more," he says.

Torben Ulrich, that great Dane of tennis, is another to whom the fineness of differentiation of muscle use is ever fascinating. It is said he can spend 25 minutes just turning a doorknob to notice what muscles he uses and what ones need be used. Differentiating. That is reminiscent of the 25 minutes of a Sensory Awareness exercise in which students take every bit that long merely to "come to standing," from a supine position—sensing, differentiating, and registering every ripple and glow along the way. And then doing it again and again.

Why so much attention to the minuscule in the quest for economy of movement? Why, indeed, the fetish for economy? In a world of fast junk food and plastic milkshakes there is no shortage of calories. There is no OPEC in that energy world. What's wrong, then, with the Papa Bear way, with the hustle and hard try? There is, after all, something to be said for overkill; at least you know that the thing, whatever it is, is *dead*.

For a start, there is that matter of repeatability. Faulty muscular tension patterns lead to unpredictability of performance. "You cannot groove your compensations." And the chances of being erratic under pressure are greater in a poorly used body. If that isn't enough to cause you to cleave to the economic, consider the laws of physics that are involved. All that excess has to go some place. It's a law of thermodynamics. The unused energy that isn't turned into movement is not simply dissipated harmlessly, evaporating into thin air. Feldenkrais tells us the worst: "It is, obviously, not lost, but remains somewhere in the body. Indeed it is transformed into heat through wear and tear of the muscles... and of the ligaments and the interarticular surfaces of our joints and vertebrae."

Clearly, more emphasis on economy of movement, on efficiency, accuracy, relevance, and sufficiency instead of excess might change the look and sound—and smell—of lots of locker rooms across the land. Gone the pungency of linament, the hum of diathermy machines, and the dour faces of tape-'em-together, patch-'em-up trainers.

The use, not the abuse, of the body is the correct study of sports.

Besides *repeatability* there is *durability*. The smooth movers in sports are the ones who hang around the longest with the fewest aches. The rough guys, however successful, fade fastest. The ones who last are the ones who do whatever they do economically, repeatably, simply. The Baby Bears shall inherit the earth.

6

THE
ENERGY
IN FEAR

"What was the means of transportation then?"
"Mostly fear." — CARL REINER AND MEL BROOKS

Sports have fears in common and sports have fears specific to them. Commonly, there is the fear of failure, the fear of looking foolish, the fear of not living up to expectations—either one's own or those of others. Specific fears include getting hit by a ball thrown like a bullet or hit by a linebacker built like a bull.

All these fears are *learned* fears,* taught from the cradle by the experience of living, but in skiing, the specific fear is with

---

*Some consider the fear of loud noises to be an innate fear, too. Those who disagree with them point out the anatomical proximity of the two branches of the auditory nerve, the vestibular, which deals with equilibrium, and the cochlear which deals with hearing. Excitation of the hearing branch, they say, spreads to the vestibular branch, and the triggered response is the same as it would have been had there been a sudden withdrawal of support—falling. The fear of loud noises, they say, is thus the first conditioned fear.

us from the timeless womb: *the fear of falling.* It is the inborn fear shared by all land animals—the loss of support, the abrupt displacement of the body in space.

From this one fear, the fear of falling, through a complexity of conditioning, come all other fears.

Some of the conditioned fears are as outwardly simple as the fear of large beasts that roar or small ones that squeak. Some are involved and socially intricate—fears such as those chessmaster Boris Spassky might have experienced in playing Bobby Fischer. He was as fearful of falling as if he were on a high wire, but the fall he feared

Nonet   ysiological responses differed only   se of a caveman beset by beasts or   . They are less appropriate to the   n brain has some antiquated stock   e otherwise the same: shortened br   ach, rapid heart rate, increased pe   flexor muscles, etc. In short, these r   ion to falling.

Anxiety is experienced as anxiety whether the threat is an action occuring in the external world or in a thought; whether it is real or imagined; and whether it is called anxiety, fear, or stress.

You can, indeed make yourself feel anxious by acting anxious, by donning the trappings of anxiety as if you were putting on a costume. Anxiety has been defined as the very experience of trying to get more air into lungs constricted by the chest muscles. Try it yourself. Struggle for breath against a tightened rib cage, tense your neck muscles, and put on the face of fear. Keep at it for a while, and you will experience an emotional response you recognize as anxiety.

You will not, however, be invited to join Actor's Studio. That group's preferred method is not to play the result of an emotion in the manner you have done, but rather to work from the inside out, to subjectively experience the emotion first. They start with the memory of a specific anxiety-making situation—a risk, a loss, a fear—and by reliving it in their imagination recreate the response, emotional and physical. If you do the same thing, you too will feel anxiety; i.e., you will struggle for breath against a tightened chest, et. al., and respond with your individually favored expression of anxiety. (Although there is a physiological similarity in all anxiety there are differences of emphasis among individuals.

Some people favor queasy stomachs, others greasy palms or buzzing heads or jelly knees, along with their changes in breathing.)

But whether you bought the box for the Cracker Jacks or the toy—you get both. Whether you start with the *physiological* response or the *psychological* response, you get both. It's a set. Since anxiety is constricted breathing, you might suspect that *the absence of constricted breathing is absence of anxiety.* You suspect correctly.

SKIING IS FALLING

Perhaps in a simpler world being afraid of something would be reason enough to avoid it. Not so. Certainly not so with skiing.

Consider that the very nature of the sport is essentially a fall, a long controlled fall from mountain top to mountain base. Perhaps in that balancing of fearful falling and controlled descent is the source of the pleasure of skiing. There are many mini-rescues inherent in every run that deliver us unscathed but still leave us in close acquaintanceship with the brink.

Is the thrill much different from that a babe in arms enjoys in a *whoops-si-do* game with its parents? *Whoops*—the downswing starts, the infant's body is tense, the breath is stilled, the eyes and mouth in O's. Swoop into *si-do*—the support firms and the gut-born giggle comes with little limbs aflail. The eyes are bright with the glow of "again." And so we glide back to the chairlift.

Unhappily, the physiological responses to a fearful stimulus are appropriate for only limited circumstances. The responses first involve sharp contraction of the flexor muscles—those muscles which bend or close the joints. With the momentary breath stoppage there comes a brief but total immobilization of the body. Perhaps in the original scheme of things, when the old part of the brain was new, this split-second rigidity under its sponsorship was a message to the attacker which said, "I'm a small thing, dead already, and obviously unpalatable."

That stage is the briefest of moments. The next response, reflexively following the sharp contraction, is the activation of the extensor muscles—those muscles which extend or open the joints. This is a state of affairs clearly of value should you decide to either lash out at your assailant or take extraordinary long strides in fleeing from it.

Meanwhile, back at the brainstem, all sorts of chemical support systems are being called into action. The heart pumps faster, blood pressure is up, even the eyes are keener. In short, you are experiencing the famous *fight or flight* response. As Mel Brooks's 2000-year-old man describes the fear-propulsion rapid transit of his youth: "An animal would growl, you would go two miles in a minute."

Alas, the fight or flight response—cued from the ancient lower centers of the brain—ill-serves modern man in his high-rise cortical world. His blood pressure elevates as of old, but now remains elevated because neither fight nor flight are apt responses. It is impolitic either to punch out his boss *or* to leg it out of the conference room—actions that would return his body to base level functioning.

Monsters no longer thunder out of the woods with a clear and present danger to the self; now they creep out of the woodwork to nibble at the self-image. But the body doesn't know—anxiety is anxiety—and its anachronistic response can lead variously to blown stacks, blown jobs, fainting, ulcers, Valium, or a ferocious net game.

The burgeoning interest in various forms of meditation, such as TM, and in Dr. Herbert Benson's Relaxation Response are ways to return the body's fight or flight responses to their baseline without actually fighting or fleeing. Competitive sports—symbolic fights—*can* be used for the same purpose, if they are not used, indeed, actually to increase the stress. Running, which is flight shod in Nikes and dressed in warm-up suits, is truly getting back to body basics.

RECLAIMING ENERGY

There is awesome energy in anxiety. Energy that 110-pound mothers have used, by more than one newspaper account, to lift a 3000-pound car off an injured child. This is its proper use, a specific, appropriate act that can be performed immediately. How satisfying that is, psychologically and physiologically. Unfortunately, most of the energy in anxiety is wasted, or subverted into polluting the ecology of the body/mind with undifferentiated tension, inflexibility, dis-ease, irritability, and hypertension.

It is possible to end that profligate waste of a valuable resource. Another valuable resource—our fossil fuel supply—is being used more fully by some electric generating plants through a technique called "re-generation" in which the previously wasted heat of their stacks is put to turning more turbines. Personal regeneration techniques could be applied to the individual. There could be recapturing of energies that would otherwise be dissipated, conscious rechanneling by the higher brain centers of the outmoded responses of the old brain. Fighting or fleeing in their gross form need not be the only choices.

The Senoi people of Malaysia, so-called primitives, learn as children how to redirect the fear they experience in dreams. They are not comforted with a "there-there, it's just a bad dream." They are told that they can intercede in their dreams as the dreams are happening and direct their course. They are taught, for instance, to turn their dreams of falling into dreams of flying, transmuting the terror of the fall into the delight of flight. As Kilton Stewart, who studied these people, put it, "That which was an indwelling fear of anxiety becomes an indwelling joy...."*

Similarly, a child's dreams of monstrous creatures—at first frightening—become through the encouragement of the parents thrilling encounters with another world not readily accessible during waking hours.

You can enter and direct your dreams too. I accidentally became an *auteur* of the night during a summer I was taking an intensive filmmaking workshop and my overloaded brain was producing dreams which all began with a clapboard—Scene 1, Take 1—*snick*. I then discovered that if I didn't like the way something was developing in the dream I could simply yell, "Cut!," reslate for Take 2, and—*snick*—start rolling on a re-dream; all without awakening, of course. Even after the movie metaphor of my dreams faded, I retained the privilege of entering them to effect script changes from time to time.

It is not difficult to enter your dreams; after all, they are *your* dreams. It just takes practice and a belief that it is possible. When next you find yourself plummeting haplessly in your sleep, be reminded of the Senoi tribe; spread your arms and soar. It is that simple, if you will trust that it can be done. Remember, *you* are the dreamer. Insist on the final cut, and thus collect the energy in any fearful dreams.

ASK HOW, NOT WHY

The first step in using the energy in fear is collecting it, not dispersing it. Trying to deny your fears, belittle them, ignore them,

---

*Kilton Stewart, "Dream Theory in Malaysia" in Charles T. Tart, ed. *Altered States of Consciousness*.

or reason yourself out of them is doubly wasteful. Not only do you lose the energy in the fear that you are trying to wall off in some understair area of your psyche, but you are losing the energy it takes to do the walling.

You do not need to figure out *why* you are fearful. (Such as, "This is the kind of snow I broke my leg in. This is the place I always louse up.") *Why* is really an irrelevant question. It leads into the byways of intellection, of "thinking about." (Head-tripping is the jargon term for it.)

How is the relevant question. How do I recognize that I am afraid? How am I holding my shoulders, my poles, my mouth? How do I change that? *How* leads to a useful, specific awareness and a "doing about."

The following conversation took place on an icy gray mountainside the third day of a Centered Skiing workshop at Sugarbush. It was a dialogue between two people, but it could be an internal monologue.

"I'm tense today."

"Is there a way you can take responsibility for that?"

"OK." (I'll go along with your *shtick.)* "I'm *making* myself tense today."

"How do you experience that tension physically?"

"Well, let's see. Tight in the shoulders and neck. Arms stiff. I'm really gripping my poles. Yeah, I'm breathing only in my upper chest."

"What's it like when you're not making yourself tense?"

"Well, more like this." (The muscles ease, the breathing deepens. Visibly, the energy settles from the high chest area, slowly following the breath down to the Center, the *tan t'ien*. The knees are less rigid, too. There is a greater connectedness to the ground.)

"Which feels better?"

"This does."

"Which do you choose?"

"This."

"OK. Shall we ski?"

"Yeah!"

Own your fears. Recognize them. Trundle them out and have a good look at them. Appraise their power and their usefulness. Take responsibility for them. They are yours; this is your script. You are the director here, too.

APPREHENSION

It is demonstrably easier and more pleasurable to ski free of excessive, undifferentiated tension. Much of that tension comes from *apprehension,* that pale shade of fear grown out of the vague anticipation of what *might* happen. More skiers catch outside edges on the catastrophic expectations against which they have steeled themselves than on any icy rut or exposed rock.

Apprehension creeps into the bones and settles in for the chill. Toes curl to clutch at the snow, fingers strangle the ski poles, and the chest tightens. All are dramatically counter-productive. No *ch'i* can flow blocked by this excessive tension. Toes turned to talons mean less contact with the boot sole, and thus less feedback from the snow's surface. Groundedness is lost. The very shallowness of the breath registers as anxiety in the brain.

Apprehension, in its preoccupation with what might happen, is future oriented, however immediate that future might be. Apprehension is a sure sign that you are not skiing in the here/now with the *is,* but in some there/then with a *could-have-been* or a *might be.*

◐

This turn, this one, is the only turn that exists. It is here. It is *now.*

The last turn, that one, however recent, is *then.* It is a *memory.*

The next turn, that one, however imminent, is *then.* It is an *expectation.*

◐

The tension between the *now* and the *then,* whether past or future, whether expressed as I-should-have or I-ought-to, is anxiety. Anxiety is shortened breath and excessive muscular contraction, and we know that skiing is best done unencumbered by such trappings.

Collect the energy that apprehension is stealing from you. Bring yourself back to the here/now. Back to Center. To get *here,* simply *be* here. Attend to specifics that remind you of where you are—your pole plant, the feel of your toes in your boots (let them uncurl), the sound of the skis on the snow, the feel of the wind on your face, and your breath as it comes and goes. Notice them.

Breathe your way back to here, back to Center.

You cannot experience anxiety unless you are breathing as if you were anxious. One is the other.

SKI AHEAD FROM HERE

"But," someone is saying, "my instructor yells at me for not looking ahead. And ski racers are taught to ski several gates ahead, aren't they? What about that?"

There is no inconsistency in skiing here/now and skiing *ahead*. The awareness of what is ahead—*there*—is experienced *here*.

Here/now is not a confinement, a dot, a black star intent on swallowing itself. Here/now is a vantage point of astounding command. It is rather like a vantage point at the top of a mountain pass that looks down on all the turnings of the road, blind curves all as you drive them, now revealed as interconnected and related. It is visibly a process.

The instructor who chastises his pupils for gluing their attention to their ski tips is merely calling for a wider awareness, whether he knows it or not. Anxiety is a notorious narrower of concentration, often to the point of fixation. The instructor is reacting to that fixation he sees in his pupil and to the anxiety he senses behind it. "Look ahead!" is just another way of saying that old stand-by: "Relax!"

Ski racers skiing a slalom course are skiing a system of gates, and in so doing are involved in a whole/parts meditation, though this information probably comes as a surprise to most of them. They are playing with the *figure* and *ground*. (See Chapter 9).

In the system they ski, there are poles that make up gates, gates that make up combinations, combinations that make up sequences, and sequences that make up the entire course. A racer's attention must be free to move instantly to the *whole* or the *part* that is the most important aspect of the system at any given moment. Free to touch on it, free to move on. Touch, move. What might be most important one moment is a single pole, a rut, or an upcoming combination. Or it might be a flashing awareness of the racer's location on the whole of the course—a monitoring of his stamina and pacing.

Touching and moving on.

But a skier on a slalom course, attending fixedly to the *there*—to a spot coming up where maybe he lost time before, is more apt to catch a ski tip on a pole *here*. His anxiety over a past performance perhaps affecting a future one has fixed his attention overlong. He has allowed it to get stuck, *there,* and it has tripped him, *here.*

Instead of being aware of the *there* from *here,* from his Center, he has tried to *be* there. Instead of sending his awareness, he has sent himself. However, until teleportation has been more universally mastered outside the sci-fi books, an orderly progression is still necessary to get us from here to there physically—these poles, these gates, taken in accepted sequence.

There are few among us who have not at some time in our lives knocked over the milk reaching for the peanut butter, muffed the ball trying to throw it before we had it, or missed the last step on a flight of stairs. All because of an out-of-Center projection to *there,* an anticipatory response to an expectation.

One's awareness, though, is free to roam here, there. It is constantly in motion and so fast in its scan that it becomes a steady state of receptivity.

That is true concentration. It is the freedom to attend specifically to the demands of the moment without *being bound* by any predetermined notion of what those demands will be, where they will come from, or how they will be dealt with. It is the relaxed alertness of the martial artists, of the Centered Skier.

Here is an exercise that might make clearer the difference between being aware of *there* and "being" there. When you finish looking at these words, look across the room at an object—a lamp, a doorjamb, something on a table. Look in the two ways I will describe and notice the differences between your perceptions.

First, look hard at the object, really hard. Focus on it fiercely. Then, as you are looking, be aware of how you perceive the other objects in the room—those you see peripherally, those intervening, and those beyond. Check, too, on your breathing.

Try it now.

Then look the second way. This time, attend to your breathing as you look. Be aware of the physical reminders that tie you to where you are—the feel of the chair, for instance, your connection to it, and its connection to the floor. When you look at the object, don't "look sharp;" look with *soft eyes,* gently. Allow the image to come to you as if you were film in a camera passively receptive to the chance play of light. Feel as if your whole body, not just your eyes, is receiving the image. Then be aware of how you perceive the other objects within your ken as you did before.

Try that way now.

Then go back and forth between the two ways of looking—sharply, then softly. "Being" *there;* then being aware of there from *here.* And notice any differences in your perception, in your breathing, and in your overall muscular tension.

If you are like those in our skiing workshops, you will notice that the soft-eyed mode, though focused on the one object, took in more information about the other objects, too, and without your trying. "It's like switching to a wide-angle lens," someone said. "The colors are more intense," said another. "I noticed things I didn't realize were there before," one of the instructors said.

Breathing was not as constricted in the soft-eyed mode, either. Muscle tensions melted with the reduced effort. Yet the object was seen as clearly *without* effort as with effort. Indeed, more was seen and sensed. So, it is clear that being where you are, being here/now, is far from limiting. It is widening of experience. It is calming and whole-making, too.

The message is: Ski *here/now,* and apprehension—that *there/then* ogre—will pilfer no more of your energy.

THE USES OF DANGER

"Dain-juh!," James Dickey calls it, his eyes snapping in his best Southern poet manner.

"If your life bores you, then risk it!" He now quotes a French writer. We were on the deck of his South Carolina house, the glint of lake water over his shoulder. I was interviewing him for a television show I did for CBS Sports on white-water canoeing—or more particularly on the phenomenon known as "The Deliverance Syndrome." People, poorly equipped for the experience, were apparently taking to white water in lemming response to Dickey's movie, *Deliverance,* and drowning.

We talked about the lure of risk, of danger. I asked him if he thought adrenalin was an addictive drug. "It is! It is!," he agreed. "But it is a benign drug, because it comes from within you."

Benign and within. There is incredibly valuable energy in the body's response to danger. Danger, immediate and undeniable, triggers a chemical cocktail popularly referred to as adrenalin. There is a time-altering jolt that comes with a rush that rivals that from any other source, natural or synthesized. The air has an after-lightning smell and the clarity of a mountain pond. Time and space swallow each other leaving no direction, no dimension. Only you in this special landscape have substance and mobility.

This is a time for *body* thinking, a time when old-brain responses are fiercely appropriate. If conflicting instructions come from higher levels, with their reasons, rationales, and their it-seems-to-me-you-should's, you'll all miss the boat.

Recognize these times and flick to automatic. It is more preservative of self.

One memorable time I did not heed that advice. In a motor race at Bridgehampton some years ago, I was certain that my OSCA could take the downhill fast bend past the pits flat out in top gear, even though that would mean altering my line there slightly to use the rough inside edge of the course. That could be tricky since the suspension system was such that the whole car could be grossly affected.

Nonetheless, I decided to try it. I will on the next lap. Well...the next lap. At last, courage to the sticking point, throttle full to the floor, I committed myself to the new line. And suddenly the bumps popped the car completely sideways... Time pulled its familiar slowdown, and I was strangely fascinated by the grain of the asphalt as it drifted toward me at the odd angle of 90 degrees. Everything happened as if underwater.

But real time still had its demands, and at that particular instant when a sharp countersteer of the wheel would have helped matters considerably, a distinct upper-level thought froze my action. "Don't overcorrect now. Don't overcorrect," it scolded. "That sand will flip you!"

Damn. I recognized the importance of a lost opportunity and the next ones presented were nowhere near as promising. (Now how bad will this be?) I slewed off the road, tripped mightily in Bridgehampton's famous sand, and flipped a few times coming to rest right side up. No breath, but no lasting harm, though I carried myself like a stack of china for the next month.

"What happened?," another driver asked me later.

"I undercorrected."

He understood.*

---

*The same accident is drawn on for another example in Chapter 8. Forgive me for recycling this crash, but I didn't have many to choose from.

When adrenalin slows the world for you, go with it; be aware you are going with it. The *movement* center is the appropriate one to handle this situation. Act now, think later. Or more correctly *reason* later. There is thinking going on—body thinking—and the body thinks best free of interruptions at those moments when adrenalin has spaced the ticks of time. Afterwards you can make logical sense of it, putting in into left-hemisphere order with the accuracy of retrospection. ("Well, I could see that the rear end had popped loose, and I knew that if I....")

DR. NIDEFFER AND AROUSAL LEVELS

I have been using the words *anxiety, tension, stress,* and *fear* in casual interchangeability to cover an entire range from mild concern to terror and to cover internal and external response. Dr. Robert M. Nideffer is far more precise and analytical. In his book *The Inner Athlete,* he discriminates among *stress, arousal,* and *anxiety,* pointing out that the three do not necessarily go together, and that different individuals have different thresholds for all three.

    Stress is the situation or the potential for arousal rather than any specific response. (The game, the race, any possibly stressful circumstance.) *Arousal* is physiological change—an increase in heart rate, different breathing pattern, etc. *Anxiety* is "psychological fear and worry."

    What is one person's stressful situation is another's piece-a-cake. A person can be *aroused* without being *anxious.* According to Nideffer, he "may worry without physiological changes occurring." Perhaps he means any obvious ones.

    Although I have some quibbles (reflected in these pages) with Nideffer's list, I think it has great value, particularly for coaches whose teams have members with widely differing basal tension levels. Nideffer calls that basal tension level the *trait* component. It is an individual's general level of tension, his *home.* Some people are simply cooler than others; some more high strung. The *state* component refers to the contribution made by a particular situation to a person's anxiety level.

    For instance, a player's *trait* component may make him Charlie Cool in a practice session, but his *state* component in actual competition may touch high numbers on the anxiety meter. I have known some technically fine skiers whose *state* component of tension in a race is debilitating. Others thrive on the pressure.

Coaches of younger competitors, secondary schools and below, and even coaches in the less jock-oriented colleges, have to deal with a far wider variety of *trait* and *state* components in their athletes, as well as a wider variety in skills. The coaches must be sensitive to these differences and adjust their coaching techniques accordingly. Particularly at those levels coaches cannot deal with all their athletes as if they were tuned to the same pitch. And yet so many do, emulating the coaching styles of the famous and notorious whose successful excesses are displayed on national TV. The Lombardis of the Little League are, unfortunately, legion. And ludicrous. What's sauce for the pros can be toxic for amateurs.

Not everyone reacts to a *stress* situation with *arousal*. Those who don't can be inattentive and inefficient. They will need psyching up, tuning. Others, generally more numerous, may have rocketed through *arousal* and into *anxiety,* as well. They will need calming, focusing.

I would put it that the latter have fragmented their energy. They need Centering. They need to collect their *ch'i* and to plug

into the universal flow. Nideffer might well go along with my metaphor since he is a knowledgeable student of the martial arts and can tell a *hara* from a handsaw. Indeed, in his book he has some advice for the many coaches who are given to heating up the stress under which their teams operate, in hopes of goading them to higher levels of arousal and improved performances. These coaches often end up with some overcooked athletes, erratic with anxiety. Nideffer suggests that instead of relying on super-psyching, the coaches look to the training methods of the martial arts. In such training participants learn to peak within the cooler ranges of optimum arousal. Relaxed/alert. Collected. *Ch'i* flowing. Centered. Grounded. Effective.

I recommend Nideffer's book for anyone involved in competition, particularly for those who like learning about themselves by answering long checklists of questions with *never, rarely, sometimes, frequently, and all the time*. The resulting graph is your individual "anxiety profile" from which you can plan a program to keep you optimally psyched. Relaxed/alert.

The Nideffer book also investigates a variety of anxiety-controlling techniques such as meditation, hypnosis, autogenesis, biofeedback, etc.—many of which I had hoped to cover in this book but do not. He also covers systematic desensitization, a valuable technique for stepping-down extreme fear reactions to levels of tolerance. It is a technique psychologists have used with success in helping fearful flyers take to the air, for instance, or in aiding people terrified of the water actually to swim. (See Chapter 7.)

PROGRAMMING FOR ANXIETY

We are riding up the chair lift on the last morning of a Centered Skiing workshop. The skier with me is a man in his late sixties who has been skiing only 6 or 7 years. He is New Hampshire to his core. "I can't ski a hill that steep," he says, carving the words in native granite. "I can't ski moguls that big." He's a strong skier, and the instructors wouldn't have him up here if they thought the terrain was beyond his ability.

"Have you ever tried?"

"Nope."

I was not going to tell this man, "Of course you can." Centered Skiing is not come-ski-with-Norman Vincent Peale. "Well,"

I said to my chair companion, "if you have never tried maybe 'can't' is the wrong word. I'd say that the only true statement you can make right now is, 'I've *never* skied a hill that steep or moguls that big.'"

Being both an engineer and a New Englander he had a built-in respect for reason and allowed that was right. We left it at that.

The upshot was he skied moguls that big and a hill that steep. He skied them well and enjoyed it.

Words have a singular power to program a response—limit it, box it, and wrap it in paper appropriate to the season. There is certainly nothing new in that, but discovering specific effects of the programming for yourself is always new. Though I grew up in the thrall of *The Little Engine That Could,* I now rebel at the manipulative and pollyannish overtones of turning *I can't* directly to *I can.* I prefer the technique common to Gestalt workshops in such centers as Esalen. There it is suggested that *I won't* be substituted for *I can't.* The resulting revelations are individual, more organic, and less imposed from without.

Here's one way the process can work in skiing.

"I can't get with it today," a workshop skier pulls up with a sigh where we wait for the video cameraman to finish with another group.

"See what happens if you say *won't* instead of can't."

"I *won't* get with it today." A smile starts across his face. "Hey, that's funny. I felt defiant when I said that. Like a small child—I won't! I won't!" He stamps his ski. "Somehow it makes me realize I *can* if I want to." He shakes his head. "That's weird." He looks down the slope where the cameraman is now waving. "Yeah," he says softly. "Yeah, I *want* to get with it today." The videotape at lunchtime proved that he had.

The transformation can be surprising. *Can't* in this context is an alas-alack word, a plea for sympathy for a put-upon me. It says, "My inability to cope with these overwhelming exterior forces is rendering me incapable of doing this. Woe and alas!"

Can't puts the responsibility for my feelings and actions out there somewhere. The plea is weakness. *Won't,* however, quickly makes clear that there is a choice involved. It says, "I could if I wanted to, but I bloody well choose not to."

Won't brings the responsibility for my feelings and actions home, accepts them as mine, and opens up the way to change. The workshop skier decided, yes, he could, after all, get with it and did.

On days when I've turned my *can't* coordinate (anything beyond the color of my ski outfit) to *won't* coordinate, I have decided that what I really wanted was to be at home in front of a fire with the *N.Y. Times* Sunday crossword puzzle and happily hie myself there.

Choice is the key. Somehow changing *can't* to *won't* makes clearer that a choice exists: your choice. Try the word on, and you might be surprised how often it fits.

There are programs built into other commonly used words, too. Programs of anxiety. Be aware of them—the *I always...*, *I never...*, *I usually...* words. Notice how you use them. See if they might not be feeding some tensions from expectations or programming into your system. Think, too, a moment, of the very word *anxiety* itself. It is a program-bearing word.

Nervous, anxious, tense—substitute *excited* for them. "I'm *tense* about the steepness of this hill, the size of these moguls," changes into "I'm *excited* about the steepness of this hill, the size of these moguls."

Anxiety is unrecognized excitement. Recognize it, collect the energy in it, and use it.

Other than the pall of apprehension and the fire of adrenalin there are various shades of fear which color skiing. Discover which are your own and decide how to collect the energy in them.

A common fear is a fear of appearing fearful—particularly for those males who are stuck like flies in the pomade of machismo. That fear can be a particularly dangerous one, warring with self-preservation and pointing a skier down slopes beyond his capability with knees twice-locked into rigidity.

Other fears, similarly dependent on the opinion of others, are fears about not having this year's "in" ski in this year's length, or this year's style of headgear or pole grips or jumpsuit. It *can* matter, if you choose for it to. Appearances do affect performances. It is said that Walt Frazier, then of the New York Knicks, always put on his shoes before donning his uniform so that he wouldn't risk creasing it. Looking cool was part of Clyde's shooting cool. Or so he believed, and action follows belief.

The risk here is that there is a dark flip side to all good-luck charms, indeed to all dependence on cues outside yourself. If you give something the power to affect you for good—whether it is a pristine basketball uniform, a rabbit's foot, or a kind word—you are giving away equal power to be affected for ill. If the charm, approval, or praise elevate your spirits, then the charm's loss, disapproval, or criticism can devastate them. Be leery, then, of giving away such power.

This is not to say that there is no energy to be collected from looking sharp, from a good-luck charm around your neck, a cheer, or a "well done!" But be aware that the energy is in your *interpretation* of these things, not in the things themselves.

So, conversely, there is energy in the *loss* of a talisman, in boos, in critical words. Such energy is less easy to collect, perhaps, because it is less appealing. It presents its negative, less recognizable face. Recognize it, collect it, breathe it to your Center where the alchemy of the *tan t'ien* can work.

And it will work.

What I am saying is that *it is all energy* — the uneasiness of being in a strange place, the self-consciousness, the irritability over the morning's minor conspiracies (the car that wouldn't start, the binding that broke). All valuable, usable energy — just uncollected, out of synch, diffused.

Catch the furrow in your brow, the working jaw, the harsh word, and the mild displeasure. Notice them. Recognize them for the snippets and shards they are — fragmented energy, ready to be made whole again. Breathe it all back into useful form and use it.

Such a reclamation system can be put to good use anywhere, anytime. At the tennis club there is a pro giving a lesson in the court next to yours. His steady barrage of racket-back, racket-back begins to erode your concentration. First, notice your annoyance. Being annoyed is one thing, *noticing* you are annoyed is another. Then recognize the annoyance as *yours*. It is your response to something happening over there, but it is experienced *here,* in you.

Then recognize the annoyance as useful energy and reclaim it. Absorb it. Take it to your Center, maybe as you bounce the ball before you serve. Then — whomp — use it.

You are in a subway station. Trains are delayed and the platform is overly crowded. You are jostled. You feel your body tighten in defense (thus increasing the effect of the jostle). Your irritation grows. Again, it is *energy:* molecules in accelerated flight under pressure. Recognize it for what it is. Don't reject the gift of energy; absorb it. Use it.

You are competing in a ski race and you drop a glove off the lift on the way to the start. A fine damn time for a thing like that to happen! Wait... Recognize the energy. You have an irritating nucleus around which you can build yourself a pearl of a performance. Collect the energy in the incident and use it.

It is *all* energy. Plug into it. Use it.

7

WORKING
WITH
IMAGES

What you see is what you get, honey!
— GERALDINE (FLIP WILSON)

*T*he BMW team sits in silence, eyes closed, in a semicircle around the team manager. On this sunny motel terrace the men are "driving" the Watkins Glen race course, mentally practicing their lines through the turns and their shift points. As each raises his hand to signal the completion of a lap, the team manager clicks his stop watch and notes that the times done in the head are comparable to the times done on the track.

The player at the free-throw line methodically bounces the ball, draining excessive tension from his shoulders and arms. Bounce, bounce. Centering. He settles his eyes on the flat ellipse that is the entry to the basket's netting. When he sees a ball there, flowing over the rim like a leaf riding a torrent down a drainpipe, he takes the ball which he holds, scoops it low, Rick Barry style—and gently *launches it on the stream to follow its image. Swoosh.*

The skier closes the chairlift bar and sighs, brushing from the full length of her right side the evidence that her just-completed run was not accomplished entirely on her skis. She lets her eyes close and turns on the replay mechanism in her head. She sees herself leaving her weight shift too late into the turn and the ski tips crossing; she feels her stiffened expectation and watches the fall. Stop. Reverse. Abruptly she whisks herself backwards out of the instantly-healing sitzmark, back around the turn to the point where the offending sequence began. Stop. Mark it.

As the chairlift carries her up the mountainside, she shoots Turn 1, Take 2 in her head. This time, she watches the timely transfer of weight, the pole plant, her body moving minimally, her edged skis pressed into a carving arc. OK. That's a print. And in the Moviola of her mind she splices the new footage in place and continues with her run—reshooting, recutting as she rides. At the summit, she slides off the chair with a smile appropriate for a skier with such a fine first run behind her.

The golfer on the practice tee pauses after each drive and closes her eyes. In her head she is watching an instant replay of her last shot, courtesy of the muscles that have just experienced it. They play it back for her faithfully. One section she returns to again and again, slowing it, stopping. There it is—in clear frozen-frame evidence; her shoulders are starting to unwind ahead of her hips. She nods in recognition and tees up another ball.

These are examples of how different techniques of visualization can be used in sports. The motor racing team is using *Mental Practice,* the basketball player is using what could be called *Instant Preplay,* the skier is involved in *Recut Your Movie,* and the golfer is her own video equipment in *Instant Replay.* These all work because of the interdependence of muscle movement and imagery.

There is increasingly clear evidence that imagery and muscles are inseparable. The "split-brain" studies of Robert Ornstein and others have demonstrated as much. These experiments involve the differing functions of the right and left hemispheres of the brain.* It comes to this: Any movement needs an accompanying image, however unconscious we are of the existence of the image. In short, no image, no movement.

---

*See Chapter 3.

Any thought, in word or image, has a bodily accompaniment also, however subtle. Perhaps the movement is discernible only on a sensitive, graph-tracing machine, but it is there.

You can demonstrate to yourself on a more obvious level how muscle activity accompanies thought. Think now of a tennis match. "Watch" the action from high up in the stands on a line with the net as two good players rally from the baseline. Settle your fingers lightly on your closed eyelids as you watch the ball go back and forth. Hit...hit...hit. Perhaps your fingers sense very little movement in the eye. Now transfer your vantage point down to net level where the ball boys crouch, and watch another exchange. Hit...hit...hit. See if you notice a difference.

MENTAL PRACTICE

In the 1920's, the physiologist Edmund Jacobsen conducted experiments in which subjects imagined themselves doing certain actions, such as running. He found that the muscles germane to those tasks showed definite contractions, small but measurable. It was clear that the appropriate neural paths were being traversed as surely as if the person were actually doing the action.

Jacobsen's findings became the basis for a number of experiments out of which emerged the fact that *mentally practicing a motor skill can be as valuable as actual practice of the skill.* One such experiment was in Australia with basketballs. In the project three groups were randomly selected, one of which practiced free throws with an actual ball each day for 20 days. The other two groups handled the real ball only on the first and twentieth days, but one of those groups, on the intervening days, had 20 minutes of mental practice—throwing free throws in their imaginations. Come the showdown: The group with no practice had not improved; the group with actual practice and the group with mental practice showed almost the same improvement.

Nearly everyone who has tried to learn a skill has some experience with the uses of mental practice. My first discovery of its value came by chance long ago when I was taking fencing lessons from Hans Halberstadt in San Francisco. One evening he was working with me on an intricate sequence with the foil involving beats, disengages, feints, parries, and counters—a veritable salad of artifice. My spirit was enthusiastic, but my hand was a stubborn puppy. I could not get it to do what it was meant to do. Hans, as was his wont when exasperated, picked up his mini-baseball bat, but even the threat of a clout could not change my doughy performance—much to my puzzlement. I was usually a quick study.

But the puzzlement proved helpful. During the week it turned my thoughts again and again to the elusive sequence, running it through my mind. Came the next session with Hans. *Salut...*on with the mask. *En garde.* And there it all was. Slick as soap. Perfect. And astonishing.

Looking back, I realize I had an accurate mental picture of the parts of the action all laid out like an easy-to-make plastic model. As I put the parts together slowly in my mind, over and over, my body was "moving," too. It was being programmed; a muscle memory was being created. Then, when my body was called upon to respond with actual movement, it did. The whole of the action was produced out of its mentally assembled parts.

But the whole of such an action cannot be treated as merely an aggregate of its parts. We know better than that about sums and wholes. The whole is, as well, *an expression of the relationship of the parts to each other.* The whole is somehow latent in each part—complete and entire—like a hologram. I had not learned a linear progression. I had tuned into a system.

In teaching motor skills there seems to be two distinct schools. One holds that you can break down the skills into finer and finer particles, practicing each bite-size morsel until it is digestible. Then you put them all together on the same plate. In the other school you learn wholes and wholes only, swallowing complete actions unchewed. (These extremes are probably recognizable to reading teachers, too).

Like any learning junkie, I have encountered in the feeding of a long habit, both techniques of teaching in varying degrees of purity.

Which is right? I answer with an old Sufi tale: Nasrudin was asked to be the judge in a dispute between two neighbors. The first presented his case and Nasrudin said, "I think you're right!." Then the second presented his case and Nasrudin said, "I think you're right!." A bystander protested. "But, Nasrudin, they cannot both be right." And Nasrudin said, "I think you're right!"

The point to remember is that the *thinking* in the doing is as important as the actual doing, and maybe more important. The difficulty arises when we assume that *thinking* is strictly an ego-bound, verbal, logical, hortatory priss who lives in the left hemisphere of the brain. Not so. Thinking can be an unmanipulative awareness, a participant in an action without being a combatant. The adversary relationship between selves is not a necessary state, it is a choice you make. Conscious direction of an activity need not be a totalitarian act, indeed, must not be if it is to be effective. Consciousness is essential to a *lasting* change in which a more effective means of doing an action — making a turn, hitting a ball — is substituted for a less effective means. "Thinking in activity" is the way philosopher John Dewey, an admirer of F.M. Alexander and his technique, put it.

In some teaching approaches that are aimed at the so-called "inner" skier or tennis player or golfer, improvement in the pupil is dramatic and almost mystical. ("Did *I* do that?") But some of that drama and mystery goes along with the charismatic presence of the teacher. Call it the Guru Effect. ("I can only do it when you are around.") The Centered Skiing workshops at Sugarbush do not depend on any individual's personality or on heightened experience for their effectiveness, although the energy level does indeed run high. Rather than a mere 5-day turn-on, what we hope for in the workshops is to plant a seed that will grow in the individual skier without dependence on any of us. That we have been successful has been attested to by most of our workshop skiers. Bill Berry, who wrote about the program for *Ski* magazine, told us the following season that it was the most enduring ski instruction he had ever experienced. It lasts because it stems from a process, a means of doing. *It is a path, not a destination.*

Means is the critical idea here. We speak of *ordering* processes (in the sense of establishing a sequence), not of *ordering* results (in the sense of demanding an outcome). These processes *do* lead to desirable results, but not results that are lusted after with an intensity that slurs the means. There is a fine interplay between wholes and parts that a fixation on outcome destroys; the too-desired outcome is then lost as well.

We speak, too, of wholes/parts and ends/means — relationships within systems. We do not mean wholes *and* parts or ends *and* means — separated and individual, as if the names named *things.* The names name *relationships,* just as the names of subatomic particles name relationships. (Do not count on actually meeting a quark one day, however charming you may be.) Wholes/parts and ends/means are named one way or the other depending on which of their Janus faces* is most important in the system *at the moment*—their particle nature or their holistic aspect.

In skiing, for instance, the pole plant is a whole action (one on which we spend a full 2-hour session in the Sugarbush workshops). It is a part, too, of the turn initiation. And it has parts: the flexion of the wrist, the awareness of Center. The whole of which it is a part is in turn a part. Thus the system flows. The names we use—whole, part, pole plant, turn—are simply a way of commenting on specific aspects of the interconnectedness of the action at any one moment. The risk is, as the risk always is, in *getting stuck* there. The risk is in putting on a capital letter, listing it in the index, and thinking of it as a noun, a thing, a Pole Plant, instead of going with the process—flowing with that unnamable which is named the Tao.

(If all this is more puzzling to you than enlightening, don't be concerned—it's only a small part of the whole.)

The Gap in the Film

When an action is imaged†—not just *thought about* sequentially, but actually *experienced* in the imagination—the same obstacles appear that appear in doing the action itself. If you really *image* a trip to the post office, it will take you as long to get to the mail box in your head as it would in actuality, unless, of course, you choose to work in distorted time (either condensed or stretched). In that case you can run a cross-country course of several hours' duration, for instance, in a minute; or you can stretch a fleeting action into attenuated slow motion.

If you image taking something off a shelf, and the shelf is too high, you will not be able to reach it in your image any more than you can in actuality. You can then call on fantasy to fly you to the shelf or stretch you there like Alice in Wonderland. Or you can stick with mundane possibility and image a stool to stand on.

---

*Arthur Koestler in *The Ghost in the Machine* also draws on the Roman god Janus to describe the two-way facing aspects of wholes/parts— which he calls "holons"—in his investigation of hierarchies.

†There is a subtle distinction between *imagining* and *imaging*. Maybe because *imagine* is used more often in its meanings of *to ponder, suppose* or *think about* and less often in its meaning *to form mental pictures* its edge for visualization has been dulled. *Image* is used as a verb, then, to emphasize the sensory replication of an event or situation in the mind.

When using imagery for learning a skill, it is important to be meticulously detailed in the picturing. Make the action continuous — as whole, as complete, as you can with as much sensory dimension as you can summon. Texture your image; hear the sounds and feel what is there to feel, taste, smell. *Be* there. Be with the whisper of the skis, the blue shadows, the cold. Hear the snow rattle on your parka; take its sting on your cheeks.

If, however, you have trouble seeing part of your action — if the film judders in the mind's projector, rips, skips, or gets stuck, that can also be instructive. *It can point up a gap in your knowing.* The message is: Your body is not completely informed (by either image or emblazoned neural path) about what it is meant to be *doing* at that particular point. To switch metaphors, it doesn't know the lyrics, so it hums.

Since the tendency is not to notice these aberrations in the film, just as you politely overlook a minor social gaffe by a friend, I ask my workshop visualizers to be particularly watchful for "missing frames" — those jumps in action in an otherwise smooth and continuous mental picturing of an action. Some important information is hiding in the miss. The missing frames are clue enough that there's a muddled message in the motor nerves — a kink in the feedback loop. There is no grooved response, just a catch-as-catch-can improvisation each time.

The frames are missing in your inner movie because your body is not clear as to what the script calls for in that sequence. It neither knows, for instance, what you *usually* do in your right turn (because you don't usually do the same thing), nor what you *should* do for a proper right turn (because you don't know). So your mental movie skips.

During a visualization exercise with a Centered Tennis group at a summer clinic, I asked both the pros and the pupils to run through their various strokes mentally. The results were instructive to all of us. "My backhand's the only stroke I can visualize all the way through," one young man said. His pro verified what I suspected: his backhand was the only stroke he made the same way twice.

The head pro came out of his reverie slowly. "I can't believe it, but that must be it," he said. In playing the movie of his serve in his head, the film kept slowing down in one place, moving frame by frame, unbidden, as if to draw his attention to something. "I could see the wrist was breaking OK, but the arm was not whipping," he said. In a tournament the weekend before he had felt his serve was off but hadn't pinned it on anything specific. "I can see and feel now that's what I've been doing lately. Actually pushing my serve." We were appropriately solemn over the vehicle of the discovery.

Some of the pros there saw their strokes as if from a camera positioned in their eyes, an entirely subjective shot. Others saw themselves as they were used to seeing themselves on videotape, an objective camera at a straight-on, medium distance. One saw his movie from a point about 20 feet over his head looking straight down on him. As you get more proficient with your built-in audio-visual equipment, you will find yourself, without conscious intent, mixing up your shots—close-ups, boom shots, tracking shots, p.o.v. instructor, the works. You may even produce otherwise impossible shots from below snow level looking up—a fish-eye curve to your skis, your boots gargantuan, and your head a tiny dot in the distant blue. Ah, yes, it can all get deliciously out of hand.

Words and Images

Knowing in words what you are "supposed" to do in a ski turn can be useful, but it is certainly not sufficient. *The weight is transferred to the uphill ski as the ski tips are eased toward the fall line, the wrist flexes to plant the pole, the body center moves laterally downhill to the inside of the turn...* For one thing, words can never describe all that goes on in the simplest actions, never mind something as complicated as sliding downhill—a process of directing and redirecting a quiverful of vectors so that the results are aesthetically satisfying as well as physically secure.

For another thing, words are left-brain dwellers, and movement in space is right-brain territory. "The part of you that can talk about it is not the part of you that can do it," my friend Gene Coghill, a talking/doing golf pro, has told me.

But words can be useful if you can translate them into the stuff of right-brained communication—images, feelings. Words are handy freeze-dried things to carry with you, but to use them you must add dimension, and swell them into space-filling wholes suitable for your purpose.

The body needs images, sensations, to act upon. Words couched in metaphors serve the purpose admirably. Metaphors are at once words and images on which the body can act. A metaphor is a bilinguist for the brain, as it were; it speaks to both hemispheres at once, verbal for the left and imagery for the right.

The architect who designed your turn may be able to describe it in precise terms; but if your body has no working drawings, no images, the muscles and tendons with hard hats and hammers will not know what to *do*. Give it an image; give it a metaphor.

Mental Practice For Racers

Every ski racer I have known uses visualization to a lesser or greater degree. Ski racing lends itself particularly well to mental practice because of the comparatively short times involved in even the longest downhill, and because of the relatively few variables. That is, the course is known and there are only one person's responses—your own—to deal with. There are no erratically bouncing balls, no teammates, and no immediate competitors. Dr. Richard Suinn, a Denver psychologist, has worked with ski racers, notably Olympic cross-country skiers Bill Koch and Tim Caldwell, using mental practice. He calls his technique *visual motor behavior rehearsal* (VMBR). Other psychologists also use mental practice or mental rehearsal effectively in skiing and other sports.

Visualization, and thus mental practice, is easier for some than for others. Imagery, our first language, usually fades as we grow up because of the social emphasis on words. The precociously verbal tots are probably the poobahs of the playground ("You be this, I'll be that) because they are most like the ultimate authority— adults— with their words, words, words.

Words become demonstrably powerful and useful in dealing with others—in overwhelming peers and in delighting adults with early evidence of socialization. Our Image Makers, in the face of this apparently superior technology, gradually fall into disuse.

Words, the noisy residents of our logical left brain, can overwhelm our quieter right-brain tenants if our consciousness is not alert. Words, so successful in dealing with the exterior world, can take over running things inside, too.

A leaf, a spiky kite, floats down to join its image on a pond. (Words inside say, "Hey, look at that leaf. Isn't that beautiful?") *The moon is a gauze of ice crystal. (Words inside say, "Wow! Some moon!")*

Though it is impossible to measure the grip words have on us, and appreciate their ability to obfuscate the silent dance of images, it is important to recognize their hegemony. Skiers in thrall to words, for instance, can believe themselves to be practicing mentally, or learning a race course, when they are only *thinking about it* in words. "Now here I must remember to keep a flat ski. Here I must keep my body low."

Remember, *images* are what instruct the body. Talk to yourself in words if you want to, but be sure that the words are translated into sight images, sound images, feeling images. That totality of sensation is what gets the race course into your body, bones, and brain—especially in a slalom course where you cannot practice or even shadow the course directly.

Slalom racers, walking up the edge of the course to memorize its path, should be certain that they *see* themselves whole in the gates: their skis where they want them to be, and their shoulders where *they* will be (if their skis are where they want them to be). Some skiers pick a line through the gates for their skis *only,* failing to visualize their entire body in action. They fail to take into account the room their body (leaning at high speeds) needs to clear the poles. Then, on their run, they are thrown off by having to adjust to a wider line—or else scatter bamboo like pick-up sticks.

In memorizing the course, slalom racers should make sure they are seeing the gates in a pattern, not in a verbal line-up: "and after the flush comes an open hairpin" etc. They must recognize the difference between *talking or thinking about* and *seeing.* They must *image.*

Good Side and Bad Side

Another aspect of mental practice for skiers I call, "Let Your Good Side Teach Your Bad Side." Skiing, like it or not, has a built-in symmetry. Until they build a perfectly conical mountain down which you can spiral in one perfect direction, skiers must turn both right and left to descend. And there is probably not a skier in the world who does not have a better turn in one direction than in the other.

In the Centered Skiing workshops we do an experiment to demonstrate how the good side can teach the bad side. I learned it from Will Schutz at a weekend workshop at Esalen. He said he got it from Moshe Feldenkrais. It might not be recognizable to either of them, now.

Here is the way we do it at a Sugarbush workshop: Stand

up with your right arm held straight out in front of you about shoulder height. Now turn your body along with your arm as you sweep it to the right as far as you can go without moving your feet or bending your knees or waist. Sighting along your finger, make a visual bench mark on the wall to note how far you have turned.

Now unwind back to where you started. Put your arm down for a moment to rest. Then do the rotation again, this time noticing where your eyeballs are as you turn. Chances are they are in the far right corner of their sockets—leading the way for your head, shoulders, and hips as you turn.

Come back to the start again. Lower your arm for a moment, then make the turn again, only this time leave your eyes behind, i.e., direct them to the *left* corner of the socket as you turn to the right. It might not be easy at first. Do that rotation, separating your eye movement from your head movement, five times. (Lower your arm between rotations to allow your muscles to send their many mini-messages.)

Then do another series of rotations, this time leaving your hips behind, i.e., twisting them toward the left as you turn the rest of the body to the right. It's not meant to feel graceful. Do it five times.

After you've done all that go back and do the turn just as you did it the first time—eyes, head, and body twisting around along with your arm—and note where your finger is in relationship to your first bench mark. If the instructions have been clear, your new mark will be distinctly farther around than your first one.

What you have been doing, as I oversimplify it, is breaking up some customary, piggy-backing neural paths to and from the brain, and thus increasing your range of motion. It is a good exercise, by the way, to include in a pre-ski warm-up.

Now to transfer some of that learning.

With your left arm straight out this time, do Step One as before, turning this time to the left and making your visual bench mark at the far extremity of your turn. Return to the front and *move no more.*

Standing in place, without moving, run through in your mind the rest of the earlier instructions, doing to the left side what you did to the right. Visualize it clearly: leaving the eyes behind; leaving the hips behind. When you have run through it five times each way as a visualization, actually bring your left arm around and again check your bench mark.

If you are like the skiers in the workshops you will be vocally surprised at the result. Your rotation to the left will be as improved, if not more improved, than your rotation to the right. Your right side has taught your left side.

The implications for skiing are obvious. Now you can spend your lift-line time or the ride up the mountain quietly replaying your good side for the benefit of your bad side. You could well end up with your bad side becoming your new good side.

INSTANT PREPLAY

Instant Preplay is a little different from Mental Practice because it happens, as the name suggests, immediately preceding the action, rather like follow-the-leader. The image does something and then you do it. The golfer watches the image ball to the cup, looks back at the palpable version and strokes it in. The weight lifter waits within his alloted time to *see* the lift, then instantly imitates it.

High jumper Dwight Stones is more articulate about his experience with Instant Preplay than most athletes: "I see a translucent image of myself coming out of myself. I watch to see if it will make it. Many times it doesn't. I have to concentrate harder.... The last time I set the record I could see two steps before I jumped that I had made it. I could see that so clearly that I even quit on it a little — almost too much."

Tim Gallwey, of *The Inner Game of Tennis* fame, whose excellent books have had major impact on the way tennis is taught and thought about, uses Instant Preplay with telling effect, although he doesn't call it that. In the serve his students "aim" at a target of a tennis-ball can by visualizing the ball hitting the can. Then they allow their bodies to put their vision into effect. If they miss the can, they take note of exactly how much they missed, allow that information to be fed into their cybernetic body mechanism, and serve again, with no conscious effort to correct for their error. Within a few attempts the ball they actually serve will be following the path of the ball they visualize, and knocking over the can.

This is the essence of Instant Preplay in all its simplicity. But to say it is simple is not to say it is easy.

The problem lies in the difference between (1) *seeing* the desired result and then attending to the process that will achieve that result, and (2) *striving* for the desired result. It is the difference between attending to the *means whereby* and *end-gaining*, to use the terms of F.M. Alexander. It is the difference between *letting it happen* and *making it happen*. And we seem, sadly, to have a cultural bias toward the more effortful way.*

Instant Preplay is most useful in those self-starting moments in sports—the tennis serve, the free throw, the place kick, the golf swing, the high jump, bowling. It is valuable in skiing, too.

In skiing, think of the turn as already existing in space in its powerful eloquence and simplicity. All you have to do is *see* it, ski into it, and put it on. See it, ski into it, and put it on, rhythmically, down the hill, shadowing with your flesh-and-blood body the vision that precedes it. (It's a game to play with space and time. But then, it all is.)

Again, putting on an existing ski turn which you *see* ahead of you is simple, but not always easy. The seeing will come and go. Suddenly it is there; grasp at it and it is gone. Even acknowledging its presence can dissipate it. Don't despair. Give it space to be there and it will be there. *Wanting* to see the turn can lead you to *imagining* that you see the turn, but that is not the same. You'll realize the difference when you actually *see* the turn.

Let go. Images are elusive and fragile and shatter from direct left-brained demands. Look soft, and you will see your turn. Then ski into it and put it on.

RECUT YOUR MOVIE

The film you recut can be a very old "movie" from childhood when you *always* struck out, *never* caught the ball, or it can be as recent as our chairlift rider correcting her first run of the day—immediately after the fact.

You can go back to those moments in your memory and re-experience the emotions that accompany the pictures. Enjoy them; suffer them. You know that. You do that. But do you know that you can also *change* those moments? You can go back along that corridor and close some doors left ajar or held ajar, and reclaim the energy now kept there as the doorstop.

How can that be? To accept the possibility of re-editing something as sacrosanct as Truth—"I mean all that is the way it actually *happened*"—is not easy for most of us. As a journalist

---

*There is more about this in Chapter 10.

I have an investment in the notion that there is a "really" which can be uncovered and reported. Facts, after all, are facts, and opinions about facts cannot change them. It's a belief system in which I function as a good reporter.

But there is, too, "a Roshomon effect" in which facts *are* as they are *remembered,* and how they are remembered depends on the rememberer's point of view — the matrix through which he perceived it at the time and the one that now filters his recall. Consider, if you've the stomach for it, all the versions of Watergate that we have had, and all that are yet to come. "Memory," Julian Jaynes says, "is the medium of the must-have-been."*

The past, then, is not *what* is remembered, but is *memory itself.* The past exists, not "back there" somewhere, but in the reconstructing and reordering in people's minds *now.*

As John O. Stevens puts it: "It is really difficult to bring home the realization that everything exists in the momentary now. The past exists only as parts of present reality — things and memories *I think about* as being 'from the past.' The idea of the past is sometimes useful, but at the same time it is an idea, a *fantasy* that I hold *now.* Consider the following problem: 'Prove to me that the world was not created two seconds ago, complete with artifacts and memories.'"**

Well...I just *know* it *wasn't....*

See, it's difficult. But the nice thing about it all is that you can if you want — like the more linear-minded in the skiing workshops — agree to act *as if* there is nothing but the *now,* and as if the past can be edited. We are, after all, not out to change recorded history, airbrushing from archival photographs the likenesses of those no longer in favor; we are just ridding ourselves of some emotional residue that clouds our view of the way we, personally, live now.

In recutting your movie, even if you cannot change what "happened," whatever that is, you can change your *feeling* about what happened. Whatever happened, happened *then;* whatever we feel about it, is happening *now.* And the *feeling* is what is important in collecting the energy you've invested in a memory.

---

*Julian Jaynes, *The Origin of Consciousness in the Breakdown of the Bicameral Mind.*

**John O. Stevens, *Awareness: exploring experimenting, experiencing.*

Recutting your movie of a distant afternoon may not, then, change the "fact" that you slipped rounding second base and got thrown out at third, rather than scoring the winning run as your recut version has it; but it will change your feeling of klutzy failure that you carry with you over that incident, a feeling that colors your present. ("I have a record of failing in the clutch." "I've always been clumsy.")

Memory erasing is the term Ruth Carter Stapleton uses for her version of movie recutting in her book *Gift of Inner Healing.* "Imagination is so powerful it can really implant the experience in you," she says.

It can. It does. In so doing it exorcises those demons of failure, turns off the power of the programming words like *always* and *never,* and allows you to reclaim energy, fragmented of old, for present use.

In a workshop called "The Tao of Sports" that I conducted one summer, the group went into their memories to recut some childhood movies. Stretched out on the floor, they relaxed the tensions in their bodies, attended to an easy breathing, and settled into a receptive state. I asked them all to reach into their memories for an incident in their childhood in some sport or game in which they had failed miserably—come in last, missed a gate, fallen, struck out, let down the team, disgraced their school, dishonored their family, etc. (The intense pressures of competition on children in our society and the natural hyperbole of childhood do not make these terms appear extreme.)

I asked the group to play their movie through slowly, experiencing it all, feeling again whatever they felt at the time— usually a string of "dis-es": disappointment, dismay, disgrace, disgust, dislike...dismal. Then I asked them to replay their movie, only this time cutting in new footage in which they changed disaster to triumph. In this footage they make the catch, hit the ball, win the race. I asked them to feel the feelings that go with that— reveling in the success and approbation, and bring it all back with them.

There was some good energy reclaimed, and some surprises for a few. One young woman said she had always hated softball, was always chosen last, was always relegated to the least active field, and was always expected to drop every ball that came her way, anyhow, and usually did. In her reverie, she went back and replayed a game; and this time she caught every fly, deftly fielded hard grounders, threw clotheslines to the right bases, and was cheered and made to feel part of the team.

On this revisiting, too, she noticed how much fun the others were having, fun she now felt capable of sharing. "It looks like a pretty good game after all," she said. "I think I'll give it another chance."

INSTANT REPLAY

The visualization technique I call *Instant Replay* can be like having your own video equipment with you. You do something; stop; ask your inner playback mechanism what did I do and it shows you. Sometimes it shows you directly, as if copied by the latest Sony equipment; and sometimes it shows you symbolically. And *that* can be fun.

I had just returned to Vermont from Big Sur in California where I had attended an Esalen workshop called "Energy Awareness" led by Bob Nadeau, the *aikido sensei*. As usual, working with Bob had pushed open not only doors, but walls, and repatterned some of my bland, blind ways of being. For one thing my Image-Maker went delightfully berserk, rather like the broom in *The Sorcerer's Apprentice*. It was nearly unstoppable and I was awash in unbidden images, some as fleeting and acceptably unreal as those in the hypnagogic world we inhabit just short of sleep. Some were simply vivid everyday pictures.

I was used to "seeing" words, often as the word itself in print (Helvetica type, quite black on shiny paper) and sometimes in cliche picture images. But now I was seeing startling pictures called up by the words—outrageous puns and nonsense images. It was like having my own personal B. Kliban drawing in my head. (He's the one responsible, if that's the word, for such mania in book form as *Cat, Don't Eat Anything Larger Than Your Head* and *Whack Your Porcupine.)*

There were memory images loosed, too. My mind was a film editor's bin with strips of unrelated footage hanging from the pins. Every so often I was treated to a quick segment of an Antonioni or Altman movie, a little Kubrick, Buñuel, Bergman, of course, and even Maya Deren! There were paintings by Magritte, Chagall, Rousseau. Klee drawings. Twyla Tharp floated by. A slam-dunk by Dr. J. and a quick 48 frames of a section of the Nürburgring race course called the Fox Röhe. It was a right-hemisphere garage sale and I thoroughly enjoyed it.

I was also at the peak of discovering the value of my Instant Replay images. And in the midst of this, golf pro John Callahan and I put together a workshop in Centered Golf at the Sugarbush course. I am not a golfer, although I have a moderately good swing—probably because it has never been under the pressure of scoring. John and I worked at the practice tee to check out the validity of my Instant Replay. I would hit a ball, "replay" it, describe what I saw—what flaws were revealed—and he would check me on the accuracy of my picture.

As it turned out there were several different ways that the inner messages were revealed in Instant Replay. One time I had a close-up, stop-frame picture of my wrists midway through the downswing. They were uncocking, straightening. I said to John, "I see I'm dissipating my power by snapping my wrists too early." He nodded. I played the mental tape through again, this time watching to see whether my wrists stayed properly cocked. When they did, I made another swing.

That was typical of one way I got the message: direct and straightforward. Sometimes that way was in close-up as it was with the wrists. Most often it was a straight-on view, as if seen by John. Sometimes, when appropriate, the view was directly over-head. I did not consciously specify the format, I just closed my eyes and took what I got.

Other messages were sent more symbolically. After one swing I saw in my interior Instant Replay an image of my legs, particularly my left leg from the knee down, as a wood carving. That was it: A still picture of a rather nice carved leg (not in the least bit bowed). The grain in the calf was lovely, like contour lines on a map, and the whole thing was finished in a soft matte glow. I admired it. The message was clear, too. "My legs are dead," I said. John nodded, increasingly intrigued by this replay mechanism I had plugged into.

The wooden leg image directed my awareness to the ex-cessive tension just above my knee. I had blocked the flow of ch'i. I worked on breaking that energy dam: Centering, attending to the wholeness of my breathing, and letting go the tension in my legs. Immediately I felt a downward rush of warmth through my lower legs, down through the cotton soles of my *kung fu* shoes (I said I was not a golfer) to deep in the ground. I was newly aware of the ground's texture and temperature. I was now grounded.

On the next shot my legs felt alive. The difference was astonishing. I could sense my left heel trigger the whole unwinding of the swing, the lower legs leading the way to a solid *whonk* of the ball. That was one fine feeling. I began to understand the appeal of the game.

So that was yet another sort of image. My Instant Replay equipment provided an obvious symbol—dead wooden leg in place of an alive flesh-and-blood energy conduit.

But the topper was yet to come. I worked my way through the bucket of balls, hitting, instantly replaying, correcting. I was getting a little cocky now. Then I hit such a hit! It had to be the largest single collection of everything that can be wrong with a golf shot. It was up and down and pushed and forced and the ball zipped off sideways into the parking lot. I went to my Instant Replay.

Image Maker, what do you make of *that!*

The Image Maker was up to it. There greeting my mind's eye was a bright green plastic 20-gallon trash can full to the gunnels with garbage! Grapefruit rinds (pink and squeezed into half moons). Melon remains. Eggshells. Coffee grounds...Garbage. I Laughed out loud. "John, you won't believe this!" He could not deny it was a singularly succinct description of the shot he had just witnessed.

What to do about it? Back to the Image Maker, and instantly—thinkable but unthought of, quite on its own volition—there appeared in all its massive, bristly pink splendor a *pig,* scarfing up the garbage. What better way to get rid of it. My reasoning left brain, given time, might have come up with the same solution, but this was a completely spontaneous message from the Image Maker.

It was perfect because there was nothing salvageable in that swing, nothing to "correct." The best way to keep its ghost from haunting future swings was to get rid of it entirely. I had. The next shot was probably the best I hit all day—any day. Clean as a pig's whistle, you might say.

During the skiing workshops we use "Let the Pig Eat That Garbage" as a reminder to get back to the *here/now.* Skiers, burdened by the tension of trying, and dogged by a string of disappointments, can cut themselves free of all that with the help of the pig. That run, that turn—it's past, it's garbage. Let the pig eat it.

I recalled that my friend, Phil Hill, the only American to be motor racing's world champion, used a similar metaphor in his driving days. "I mailed that letter," he would say, and any error was forgotten, its power to interfere with his concentration now ended. It's a good image. Drop a letter in a corner slot and it is out of mind.

Until your own Image Maker comes up with a more personal image, feel free to use either of these to clear your present of past programming. Let the pig eat the garbage; mail that letter.*

SYSTEMATIC DESENSITIZATION

Images are at the core of a technique devised to modify the behavior of people with specific anxieties or phobias. The technique, called Systematic Desensitization, combines deep relaxation with the visualizing of certain fearful situations arranged in a progressive hierarchy, such as in the example below. The technique was developed by Dr. Joseph Wolpe, a behavioral therapist, and is used by many psychologists and psychiatrists to treat subjects who are afraid of cats, afraid of elevators, afraid of flying, afraid of the water, etc.

Dr. Robert M. Nideffer, author of *The Inner Athlete,* has applied the technique to the fears in sports with measured success. Desensitization can be used to rid injured athletes of any residual fears they have that might affect their future performance. A batter who had been beaned, for instance, might no longer be so keen on digging in at the plate. A football player who had been blind-sided once too often might shy from the sound of pounding cleats.

I make the point in Chapter 6 that you cannot be anxious and relaxed at the same time. The two states are mutually exclusive. And that's the simple foundation on which Systematic Desensitization is built.

Here is the technique as it might be used in skiing, say for a skier who can only smile wanly when others sing of the glories of deep powder snow. (He had deep snow to thank for a green-stick fracture of the tibia a dozen seasons ago and still is leery of it.)

---

*Maybe these two metaphors have more than casual connection. I am suddenly reminded—by an image of where it appeared on the page— that the "all-universal principle of living" as promulgated by Gurdjieff in *All And Everything* deals with similar subject matter. The principle: "If you go on a spree, then go the whole hog including the postage."

With the therapist, the skier agrees on a hierarchy of situations with ascending scores on his anxiety meter. Such as:

- Seeing a cover picture of *Powder* magazine that shows a skier moving in a mantle of dandelion-seed snow.
- Hearing a weather forecast on the car radio predicting heavy snowfall on the way to a ski weekend.
- Overhearing people in the base lodge discussing how deep the powder is on a particular run.
- Riding the lift on the way to that trail looking down on the tracks in the deep snow below.
- Standing at the top of the trail with a skier behind saying, "After you."
- Watching a good skier take a bad fall in the deep snow just in front of you.
- Starting off down the slope and watching your skis, and then your boots, disappear in the deep stuff.
- Feeling your invisible skis begin to part company and go their individual ways into a split and a certain fall.

Using a deep relaxation technique (such as Progressive Relaxation, Relaxation Response, or biofeedback) the subject relaxes as completely as possible and visualizes the least threatening scene on the list. If he experiences even the least evidence of anxiety—often recognizable first as a change in breathing—he stops the visualization, and attends to deepening the relaxation. Then, again, back to the visualization. And so on, until he can handle that situation with, literally, no sweat. One down and on to the next most anxiety-making level.

Eventually, the subject will be able to go through the entire hierarchy without experiencing anxiety. And, ideally, he will be able to carry that calm with him into the teeth of the storm when it is met in reality.

ASK YOUR ENERGY

The Centered Skiing workshop instructors thought I had really slipped over the edge this time. It was a pre-season session and I had something to share with them. John looks at me with his mouth slightly agape. Martin's head is cocked to one side. Peter has that look that says we must be having language difficulties. And Bucky, who had rented my studio to live in the season before, seems to have decided that he had been right all along: the land-lady is dingy. Still, they are going along with it.*

I ask them to "settle" into their energy body and take hold of the chair they were standing behind as if to lift it. "Set-t-tle, set-t-tle." I could hear Bob Nadeau's soothing sibilance suggest the same thing in my memory of the workshop with him. At Esalen, in the hall called Huxley, we all held one of the ubiquitous giant cushions which are the furniture of that realm and, se-et-tling into ourselves, had "asked our energy" how to lift them. And most of us had after a time been rewarded by mental images which directed our bodies to the least effortful way to complete the task; i.e., lift the cushions. What came were symbols of easy lifting that were messages both from and to our bodies — images which are always there, like television signals in the air, but un-noticed unless we tune in to them.

Bob's workshop involved practice in tuning into the myriad of images, full of information and direction, which surround us and to which we are usually oblivious. The "off" button is perenially pushed.

In the Wunderbar at Sugarbush, where we hold the morning sessions of the Centered Skiing workshops, there are sturdy cap-tain's chairs, not cushions, so I ask the four instructors to each stand behind a chair ready to lift it, and se-et-tle into his energy, into his Center, and notice any image that comes to him.

Don't look for an image, don't either expect one or not expect one. Don't *do* anything; just *be* there. Images are shy, reticent. They are dubious, now, after years of being ignored in favor of the talkative left side of the brain, which quickly pipes up with: "Flex your knees. Lift with the large muscles of the leg. Protect your back from strain."

Set-t-tle.

Breathe into your Center. When the image comes, you will notice it more in the having-been-there. Trust it. Let it sidle into your ken without having to bear the brunt of your full attention. A stray dog will ease to your quiet hand and shy away from the slapped thigh and the "Here, boy!"

Nothing.

The looks.

---

*The instructors whose bare first names, like the names of saints (which they are in their way) are scattered throughout this book, have last names too. They are: Peter Forsthuber, Bucky Makowski, Martin Marnett, John Nyhan.

The four instructors are standing, slowly lifting the chairs and setting them down, lifting and down. Then the expectancy and the watchfulness start to shift subtly to simple receptivity. They are waiting now, just waiting the way mountains wait.

Martin's face lights up. "CO_2 cartridges!" he says. He is pleased. "There was suddenly a CO_2 cartridge in each leg of the chair. When I lifted, pow! They fired!" And when they fired the chair was easier to lift; it rose with less muscling, less effort.

Now the images are more readily noticed. We are all visited by them and offer them for discussion: forklifts, derricks, helium balloons, hydraulic jacks. All spontaneous images to help in the given task, here, now, of lifting a chair. And the lifting *is* easier. Everyone agrees to that, even in the regular workshop sessions later in the season: If you have an image, the task is easier. The pooh-poohers wave it off. Ah, that's just your imagination.

Precisely!

In search of an explanation one might suggest that the image of assistance has allowed us to cut back on the excess of effort we usually assemble when faced with a task. Since we have "outside" help, we have cut our own input back to bare necessity. Lifting the chair *seems* less effortful because it *is* less effortful; we have put less effort into it. We have differentiated out the superfluous and the redundant muscularity, accepting in its stead the generous aid of imaged forklifts, and CO_2 cartridges.

We can experience a similar feeling of ease in action when arising from a chair, for instance, if we image a large balloon attached to our heads lifting us up. Give your body an image to act on and allow your body freedom to act on it, and you will be more economical in your moving.

However, there is an important difference between a consciously created image and an image that appears spontaneously when we settle into our Center and "ask our energy."

What is the difference? I think it is that the conscious image is a message *to* our bodies, whereas the spontaneous image is a message both *from* and *to* our bodies. It is a more knowing image, a more complete metaphor. With the conscious image we impose on our bodies an order from central headquarters, the brain. With the spontaneous image we incorporate into it feedback from the distant outposts of the nervous system as well. The spontaneous image knows what's going on in the hinterlands.

I think you'll be happier with an example.

I noticed in the workshops that the lifting images that were reported were always particularly appropriate for that person's body and body condition. One man, whose image was of a weight lifter doing curls, had powerful biceps and forearms and could easily raise the chair by curling it. A young woman, slightly built, had been struggling to lift her chair with bent arms and upper body tension. She reported no image; no, no image yet. Suddenly she relaxed and the chair seemed just to swell off the floor. She looked astonished. "What was your image?" I asked her. "Nothing, really," she said. "Well, wait a minute. There was this balloon thing under the chair...." She had exhaled to fill it, her body had eased, and the chair was lifted.

There was one skeptic, proudfully logical, who believed well enough that you could *image* an image, but to have one appear unplanned for? Nevertheless, he agreed to make room for it. He, too, suddenly changed the way he was lifting. He had been tentatively moving the chair about, but now his knees bent and straightened with his upper body perfectly erect, and the chair rose authoritatively. "A large worm gear right under the seat," he said sheepishly. I suggested that the straight up-and-downness of his image might be telling him that there was a potential weakness in his lower back. He shot me a look. "I do have a bad lower back."

Thus, workshop after workshop, I became increasingly convinced that a spontaneous image—being in touch with your entire body—can not only bring a possible trouble spot to your awareness, but it can also direct you around it to the completion of your task. It's a built-in how-to-do-it-better guide with a self-protection feature. It's a handy gadget to have.

Indeed, I used mine again a few minutes ago. Having decided to avoid finishing this chapter by pruning the apple tree, I managed to get myself, literally, out on a limb. The excitement of the chase had worked me out too far, and getting back wasn't going to be easy. The terrain dropped away rather sharply below. Getting down, I realized, was not going to be as simple as it would have been a quarter century earlier. There is that way of placing your hands beside you on the limb, pivoting and swinging down to drop to the ground. But, that would mean going from a bent arm to a straight arm rather abruptly, and my right elbow had been paining me for months (an excess of improper use having caught up to me).

So. "Ask your energy."

There were several rapid images all telling me to keep my elbow straight throughout. In one version, my arm was in a heavy cardboard tube, like a mailer. In another it was baked in a crust like a Beef Wellington. But the operative image was one of those hanging wooden monkeys that Danish furniture stores import by the windowful: straight arm, cupped hand, and articulated shoulder. Monkeys know more about trees than anyone. I acted on it; leaning far out to a limb opposite, hooking my (wooden) hands over it (with unopposed thumb, I noticed) I swung down on my straight arms. I felt not the slightest elbow twinge. And here I am, back at the typewriter, smug as hell.

The capacity to visualize is in all of us—recapturable by practice, if you refuse to let words and linearity limit your gallery. *Seeing With the Mind's Eye* by Mike Samuels and Nancy Samuels, and Robert H. McKim's *Experiences in Visual Thinking* are good places to begin widening your internal vision. So is *Put Your Mother on the Ceiling* by Richard de Mille.

But look, all I want to do is stop stemming on my right turn!

Believe me, it helps to open yourself to images. See red frisbees, glockenspiels and gold velvet chairs, popsickles, winged horses and needle-nosed pliers, striped spinnakers, winged serpents, thick-pile carpets, and toasted marshmallows. See things—real things, fanciful things; even a right turn without a stem. There are continuous showings in the magic theater of the mind. And there's *always* a cartoon.

8

BREATHING

*Think of yourself and feel yourself as
a breather.*   **— FRITZ PERLS**

"Now breathe in dandelion seeds." I see Peter's nose twitch, avoiding a sneeze. "Let the seeds float around inside. Now breathe them out....Now breathe in tiny marshmallows.... Now out...." Now thumbtacks. Now rose petals (a soothing favorite).

An off-slope session of a Sugarbush Workshop in Centered Skiing is underway. We are playing a variation of a game called "Breathing" from Robert de Mille's delightful book *Put Your Mother on the Ceiling.** Eyes are closed. Everyone turns inward to check how it feels to have dry leaves whirling around inside the chest, or tiny unicorns or chocolate-chip bits. (A sudden smile. Later we learn that the happy breather had found some tiny marshmallows

---

*Published by Walker and Co., now a Penguin paperback. As so often happens I met this book through another one I like: *Experience in Visual Thinking* by Robert H. McKim.

left over to combine with the chocolate chips.) Besides such sweet serendipity the breathing game has practical purposes. Here are some of them:

1. Practice in visualization.
2. Practice in breathing.
3. Practice in anxiety awareness.

Practice in visualization. As we see in Chapter 7, our image-making mechanism has been stored in basement dampness too long for easy operation. It needs the oiling of use. Images are the language of movement, so we must do our flash-card drills to improve proficiency. The breathing game can be just such a drill. The sharpness of images is not as important here as the willingness to be imaginatively free, to unplug the monitoring of our left-brain logic—"You can't breathe gumdrops!"—and do what we choose to do.

Practice in Breathing. The game allows us to be aware of our breathing, but *indirectly* aware, avoiding the temptation to manipulate it, to try to do it "right." What could be more free of *shoulds* than breathing candle flames or lightning bugs? There is no *right* way to take in a lungful of mini-motorcycles to pop-pop about in your chest. Yet, as we are inhaling such things, we are at the same time attending to the filling of our lungs; we are, without intending to be, more aware of the process of breath.

Practice in Anxiety Awareness. Anxiety is only a label we tie to troubled breathing (see Chapter 6). In this game, we are dealing with how we *make* it troubled. How *we* make it troubled. The game is good practice in taking responsibility for that troubling, in accepting that we are the troubler as well as the troubled. Anxiety-producing clues can come with equal effect from either inside or outside us—from the reality of a threat, or the fantasy of a threat; from a threat that is really real, or a threat that is perceived as real. The breathing game helps make the distinctions clear.

In our breathing game we find that the foreign matter we are breathing is not so foreign after all. We can domesticate it, if we choose, by breathing it in. We can welcome it inside the intimate chambers of our respiratory system. With inhalation we have thus converted a *that* to a *this*, an *it* to a *thou*. Like Jim

Henson with his monsters of Sesame Street, we have Muppetized our anxiety-makers until they are merely odd and scratchy, but no longer menacing.

The existential message is breathe it in and it is yours.

TENSION IS A CHOICE

In skiing, we choose to put ourselves in a predicament as alien to our nature as breathing thumbtacks. We willingly stand poised on two waxed slivers at the tilting brink of a snowfield. A forbidding landscape for a warm-blooded, survival-oriented organism. But we have chosen the site. We know that. If our chest constricts at the prospect of it, we have chosen that constriction, too. We must recognize that we have chosen it. Our game of breathing tacks or goldfish has taught us that we can breathe it in or not. We can continue to experience—or not—that chest constriction we variously call anxiety, fear, or stress.

To be anxious or not to be, that is the decision, and you can take a reasoning role in making it, if reasoning is your way. Thus: Is it a real threat (say, inhaling water), and is the threat real? (Is real water being inhaled?)

Is it a real threat (falling 2000 vertical feet), and is the threat real? (Is it reasonable to assume that a skier with your ability, in your condition would be unable to handle such a slope?)

Is it a real threat (slamming into a firmly rooted fir tree), and is the threat real? (Is the trail so narrow and snow conditions such that the risk is unacceptably high?)

If you decide that what you face is not only a real threat, but that the threat is real—act accordingly. If you are, for instance, submerged in water, *don't breathe.* If you are facing a gash of a ski trail beyond your ability or conditioning, *don't ski it.* Seek out alternate routes down the mountain; perhaps the lift that brought you up.

But if you choose to ski the trail, then choose *not* to let anxiety infringe on your ability to cope with any real threats to your well-being. A tension-locked downhill knee cannot serve you well in a mogul field; shoulders rigid with watch-it are no help in the glades. Remember that the fear of what might happen can make it happen.

Before you push off, collect the energy fragmented by your tension. Collect it by breathing it back to wholeness. Breathe your negatives into positives. Breathe your way back to Center. Breathe.

BREATH AS ORGANIZER

You cannot *not* breathe and survive for long. If you are without oxygen for 8 minutes a critical part of you dies forever. Compare this with how long you can live without water, without food, or without the touch of a loving hand. But breath is more than an errand boy bearing oxygen. Breath is the organizer of the organism.

Notice it.

Breath is both beacon and bellwether. It lets you know when you are off course, out of kilter, uncentered. It can lead you back, as well. Back on course, back into kilter, back to Center.

Notice it.

Breath catches in your throat. It is small, furtive. It comes only upper-chest deep. You feel enclosed, tentative, vaguely uneasy, out of sorts.

Now open a way for the breath. Release the bands you have lashed around your chest. Ease the grip on your belly, your back and your sides. Allow your breath its fullness. Let it flow, ebb, flow.

And as you do, notice it.

Let its mending ways have their way. Let your breath knit you back together. Let it realign you with the benign aspect of gravity. Let it tune you, putting you in harmony with the universe. It can do that. *Ch'i,* the Chinese character translated as *energy,* is *ch'i,* the very same character translated as *breath.*

Be a breather and be breathed.

"Notice your breathing," I say to a group of eighty ski instructors. It is not easy merely to allow breathing to happen, watching it as if it were a golden carp in a pond, without yielding to the urge to *do* something about it.

"Don't do anything to change it for now; just observe its coming and going." Within a few breaths' time we have to laugh. Such a held hush comes to the room, such an obvious *trying* in trying not to change anything. Some solved the dilemma by simply not breathing at all. It was like asking a roomful of centipedes that fateful question about the order of their locomotion.

Maybe we have too often been asked to notice something when noticing was not what was wanted. *Change* was wanted. For instance, when your mother asked, "Where are your feet?" she was not seeking anatomical information. She was saying, "Kindly take those dirty sneakers off my clean slipcovers." Surely, then, when someone asks, "How are you breathing?" we are certainly being told to change our errant ways. Hastily we flip through all the schoolroom admonitions to sit up straight, pull in the chin, stick out the chest, take a deep breath. The urge to do it *right,* whatever that is, is strong. We are eager to comply with either someone else's notion about correct, or to impose a previously learned one of our own. To control. To affect. To manipulate. Our buttons have been pushed, and we are instantly hard at it—gaining ends instead of attending to the means.

BELLOWS AND BALLOONS

Lungs are odd things. Mismatched in size (the left one having to share office space with the heart), they are highly elastic. When the muscles of the diaphragm and the chest area pull the furniture out of the way, they expand to fill the space left. Since the lungs stretch in size when filled with air, the temptation is to think of them as balloons—inflating, deflating. But lungs are lumpy, spongy things, filled with clusters of tiny air cells—not at all smooth-walled like the balloons you buy at the circus and pop with a pin or twist into animal shapes. Yet it appears, in my observation of breathers, that most people fill their lungs as if they thought of them as balloons.

Take a deep breath.

When I ask workshop skiers to do that, I find that most of them take a *big* breath rather than a *deep* breath. And "big" is a more apt description of the muscular effort involved than of the volume of air actually taken in. Indeed, such Herculean efforts at breathing result in a relatively small increase in lung capacity.

Take another deep breath. For many people taking a deep breath involves expanding the upper chest hugely, shoulders lifted toward the ears, nostrils collapsed against the awesome suction, and throat cords pulled taut. Maybe the stomach is tensed, too. Actually, the fiercely contracted muscles involved in the effort have delimited the expansion of the lower areas of the lungs. And the lower areas have the greater potential for expansion. All that effort at breath-taking has resulted in only a moderately bigger, upper-chest breath.

Take another deep breath, and this time think of deep as a *place,* not a size. Let the lower areas fill as well as the chest.

Chapter 8 Breathing /105

And let the *back* swell, too. Breathing is not something to be done only in *bas relief*.

Maybe the trouble lies in the balloon image. Such an image pictures the lungs as something in need of being blown up, something requiring the forcing of air into them. An active step that demands sniffing at the air with determination to fill those limp rubber sacks.

Forget the balloon and picture a bellows.

Open a bellows and air rushes in. You are hard put to keep it out, since we live in air, and ubiquity is its nature. Open your chest and diaphragm like a bellows and air will rush in. Nature abhors a vacuum, no less in your thoracic cavity. *Taking a breath, therefore, is really accepting one.* Attend to the essential conditions — i.e., create the space — and ye shall be breathed.

THE YOGI'S GREEN CARPET

I had been breathing for a long time before I had any lessons in it. Then, some 20 years ago, I sat in a pained approximation of a Lotus position on Majumdar's grass-green carpet in Manhattan's Upper East Side and took up breathing seriously. One thing was instantly clear to me — I breathed in a far different manner than a yogi did. I was working at breathing; Majumdar was a breather. I was blowing up balloons; he was a bellows. I made a sniffing sound when I breathed; I heard none such from him. I felt the sucked-in wind of the breath in my nostrils; I wondered if he felt it in his. Nothing was said; I breathed and watched him breathe. Then it happened. I felt the *passage* of air in my nostrils, not the *effort* of sniffing at it. I felt the impact of the air in my *throat*. Deeper, easier. And the noise changed to a deep-sleep sound, a soft distant roar as the air rushed in, pulled in from deep in my Center, not sniffled in by surface effort. I was beginning to be a breather!

My discovery of effortlessness in breathing stood me in particularly good stead some years later when I was racing cars. I managed to go off the course at Bridgehampton in an uncollected manner and flip over. It was an open car, and with only a lap belt to hold me, I flopped around enough to get solidly whomped in my upper back, knocking all the air out of me. As the dust settled and a clutch of hands came at me to tug at my helmet and seat belt, I wanted nothing but a deep draught of air. But gasping would have been far too painful for my chest. Inside me was a calmness saying, "When you really have to breathe, you will." I saw the green carpet and there came an easing in my stomach muscles, making a space. I heard the welcome rush in the throat as the air streamed past the held-still ribcage. And then, having the air to speak, I said, "If you'll unfasten my helmet first, it will come off easier."

Perhaps my saving yoga breath would have been more appropriate had I been driving a Lotus. Alas, it was an OSCA.

PRODUCING, HELPING, PREVENTING, ALLOWING

Charlotte Selver, that gentle person who developed the body/mind technique known as Sensory Awareness, has distinguished among *producing* breathing, *helping* breathing, *preventing* breathing, and *allowing* breathing. It can be instructive to notice which word best fits the way you breathe in various circumstances: sitting in a traffic jam, overhearing an argument, balancing your checkbook, waiting for someone to judge something you have done. Helping, allowing, preventing, producing. Which is it?

In an on-slope session of the Sugarbush workshops, John noticed how all his pupils *prevented* breathing for that small moment just as their skis turned into the fall line. He also found that by having them consciously *produce* breathing at the critical moment, they eased past the mini-crisis. And, of course, since the prevention of breathing is tension, the production of breathing eased that tension enough for the skier's performance to improve. Soon they were confident enough to *allow* breathing right through the fall line.

Looking for that little catch in the breath at the fall line is an easy way to check the anxiety level of the moment. Anxiety means undifferentiated tension and restriction of flexibility and ease, which limits a skier's ability to *go* with the mountain. Look for that...catch. Your breath is a sensitive gauge to how freely all systems are flowing.

"Be aware of your breathing," we suggested to the workshop skiers. "Don't do anything about it for now. Just be attuned to the nature of it as you ski." One man was vehement: "I can't ski and breathe at the same time!" We all laughed. But he was right. He did his damnedest to avoid breathing and skiing at the same time. He would have been perfectly safe skiing under water. But he found that by *attending* to it he could, after all, deal with both, awkwardly at first, then more easily. He found, too, he could make more turns before he had to stop, and better ones, as he breathed himself to Center.

Awareness can have a liberating impact.

Ski racers and other competitive athletes have long known of the difficulties of *allowing* breathing in the stress of action and often *produce* breathing in a ritualistic pattern to make certain they do it. Muscles need oxygen for contraction and performance suffers quickly without a steady supply of it.

When I was covering ski races for the *New York Herald Tribune* I always knew when Olympian Tommy Corcoran was on the slalom course. I could hear the patterned *woosh!* of his exhalations long before he was near. Um *woosh!* Um *woosh!* His breathing technique not only assured him of oxygen in constant adequacy, but also established a metronomic rhythm against which his skis played. He was a breather, particularly an exhaler.

Golfer Chi Chi Rodriguez is another noisy exhaler. He believes his outrush of air on his drive add yards to its length. Jimmy Connors' tennis strokes come equipped with sound effects. And most dramatic of all is the *ki ai* yell of martial artists, exhaling on attack, and freezing their frightened adversaries in their tracks with curdled blood. (Or at least that's the way it happens in my favorite *kung fu* movies.)

But to the more casual breather, exhaling seems to be the stepchild of breathing. A breath to many breathers means *inhaling*. Ask them to hold their breath. They probably hold it on a full inhalation. Ask them to count their breaths. Wherever they are on the cycle, chances are they wait for the next inhalation to count *one*. And further, ask someone to help you move the piano or heft a heavy box onto a table. Again, its a fair guess that the person will inhale sharply, probably even holding the breath while doing the deed.

Those who know say you should *exhale on effort,* inhale on release. In doing push-ups, for instance, exhale as you push up, inhale as you lower the body. That's the advice West Point cadets get from Col. James L. Anderson, director of the Physical Education Department and co-author of *The West Point Fitness and Diet Book*. Colonel Anderson points out that it can be dangerous to hold your breath during extended effort, such as in a series of exercises. The held breath sets off a series of physiological responses: first the arterial blood pressure decreases, then the heart rate increases and the blood pressure rises—particularly in the arteries to the lungs. A previously undetected weakness there could be revealed disastrously.

While doing my frequent winter meditation, called shovel-the-snow-the-plow-dumped-in-front-of-the-garage, I pondered the matter of death by snow shovel, a not uncommon occurrence every winter in the north country, and came up with a theory I reveal here for the first time. I believe that those who expire while shoveling snow (and pushing stuck cars) are overly concerned about getting the job done and are not attentive to the way they are doing it. They are *end-gaining* instead of attending to the *means whereby*, to use F.M. Alexander's phrases. In so doing they are probably holding their breath and too, not exhaling on effort; they are not harkening to the internal messages; they are over-taxing their systems. They have put themselves on *manual override*, and they are dying. End of theory.

FELDENKRAIS EXERCISES

Exhaling on effort might not seem natural to you. Just another rule, another order to pass on to the overburdened troops.

Has Feldenkrais exercises for you!

Feldenkrais exercises are unlike any you have ever encountered, particularly if the word *exercise* strikes images of effortful one, two, three-ing. Moshe Feldenkrais is a creative mover and thinker from Israel who came to his theories of movement in a most unscientific manner—that is to say not through the research channels cheered by academia (for one thing, he is a physicist, not a physiologist), but through his own experiences. As a soccer player in his youth, a black-belt Judo instructor later, and still later as an innovative rehabilitator of war-distorted bodies in Israel, he evolved his notions and his thousands of exercises.

Feldenkrais exercises are designed to lead people to an increased awareness of how they move. Not how they think they move, not how they ought to move, but how they *do* move. Many of the exercises—really adventures in discovery—are published in his book *Awareness Through Movement,* but a more direct way to experience this remarkable man is in a collection of cassette recordings which supplement the book.*

Click a cassette in place and Dr. Feldenkrais's rich accents

*Lessons from Moshe Feldenkrais. Awareness Through Movement, Westinghouse Learning Corp. Training Systems, Pittsburgh.

lead your body in a series of wondrously simple movements, in slow repetition at your own speed, allowing time to sense what is happening. An exercise may be no more than lying supine on the floor and slightly raising an arm or leg. Sensing. Repeating. You are narrowing your attention to the quiet messages that your body parts are constantly sending. It can be like suddenly hearing bird song over traffic sounds as the body tunes to the more subtle sensations usually lost in the clangor of gross movements. Sensing. Repeating. The body on its own hunts for the direct way, as a small boat hunts to hold a course.

Gradually, marvelously, the body selects the way it prefers to move. There is satisfaction, an ease in doing, a rightness which has that quality engineers call "elegant."

Quite likely you will discover that, yes, you want to exhale on effort, but the decision will come as an internal revelation, a plebiscite of the proprioceptors, as it were, not a fiat from an external authority.

It might be interesting to speculate why the intake of air has come to seem more important than its output—why *inhale* has come to mean breath and exhale is something that tags along—but it is more worthwhile to disabuse you of the notion. Tom Corcoran's effort was well expended on the *woosh* of exhalation. He knew that if he expressed the used air from his lungs, new air would replace it as certainly as he knew his skis would carry him down the mountain, not up.

While attending to your breathing, then, when anxiety has laid its hand on you, it might be helpful to start with an exhalation. There is used air (carbon dioxide) to expel, as well as oxygen to be taken in. One is as important as the other. The *exchange* is critical, the *balancing* of carbon dioxide and oxygen—not the intake of air for the sake of air. You do not need a breath so much as you need breathing. Breathing is, as everything is, a cycle, a loop.

And do not, in your haste to take in air and push out air (or push out air and take in air), overlook that peaceful plateau in the cycle which is neither breathing in nor breathing out—that moment *in between* that is freed of all necessity. Turn your attention to that small still glade in your breath—that brief Bardo. Allow it ever more space in your breathing. Nurture it.

Thus do you become a breather.

9

LEARNING

Abandon learning and there will be no sorrow.   — LAO TZU

A click, a lightbulb, Eureka, aha! However we have experienced it, we have experienced it: That bright moment when we have *learned* something, when a joining has happened and we are changed.

Yet we tend to look upon learning as acquisition, as adding to an existing fund of knowledge as we would add to a shelf of books. We think of what we learn as something separate to us, and we annex it. We go to school or take lessons to "get" something, adding ever more to our cache, stockpiling and collecting. Wisdom, in that case, must be a curiosity shop with sagging shelves and overflowing cardboard cartons.

Behind these actions is the notion that there is an *it* to get, or a *there* to get to. (I haven't got it yet, but I'm getting there.) Thus do we put ourselves under the tension of searching out, acquiring, and adding to. Our brow furrows, our neck tenses, and we direct our fierce attention outward, ever fearful of missing something. And thus do we miss it; for what we are looking for is not *outside;* it is *inside,* awaiting discovery, awaiting awakening, awaiting the spark that reveals.

Learning is not adding on; learning is paring down. It is destroying old patterns; it is reordering and reconnecting. Learning is replacing a complicated, less complete way with a simpler, more encompassing way. It is seeing the picture more whole.

You know everything you'll ever know; learning merely brings it into awareness. Whether or not that is true does not matter, since if you act *as if* it were true, learning becomes less

pressured, more relaxed, and thus easier. If you approach learning to ski as if there existed within you the Perfect Skier waiting to be freed, as a sculptor frees a statue with his chisel, then the anxiety of acquisition fades. You touch the learner in you, and you learn. Instead of looking upon lessons as the tedious annexation of new skills, look upon them as an opportunity to slough off what is encumbering you, a chance to rid yourself of the excesses of the old ways, and clear the debris of faulty habits from the wellspring.

Learning does not stem from do this or don't do that. Learning stems from *what happens* when I do this or don't do that. Notice what happens as you move in different ways. If you like what happens (your skis stay effortlessly close together, for instance) then continue to do what you did. Attend to the process and the desired result will follow—like grass grows, like moon rises.

Any trouble comes from jumping to the result, from *trying* to keep your skis together, from wanting the moon to leap to its zenith. Attend to the process, the *means whereby,* and the result will follow; attend to the result, straining for it, and you get neither the process nor the result. And yet *suggest* the result, lightly, through interior image-bearing channels—not through exterior verbal demands—and the proper process will find you.

The monkey wrenches in the works are *effort, tension, trying, hanging on, and getting stuck.* Relax, pare down, let go, and simplify. Chuang Tzu speaks of "the fasting of the mind." Let the mind fast, and learning happens.

THE MYTH OF THE CHILD

A cliché of the ski slope is a tiny child, head bulbous with crash helmet, whipping by as we smile, shake our heads, and share our "if onlys." The implication is if we adults were not handicapped by the very nature of being adults, we, too, could ski like that. Look again. Do you want to ski like that? Knees locked in a straight-legged snowplow, sitting deep with your bottom barely clearing the bumps? That, after all, is the way most small children ski.*

When I was a child I spake as a child, I understood as a child, I thought as a child; but when I became a man, I put away childish things.

That chapter from Corinthians can be read as a sad loss of innocence, an irreversible corruption, or it can be read as growth:

---

*I'll except Patrick Lonsdale. My editor excepts his son, Anson. You are allowed one exception of your own, age 6½ or under.

a moving on from what was *once* appropriate to what is *now* appropriate. "Learning like a child" has been held out to us as the key to some lost golden kingdom of perfectability; but a child learns like a child because that is the only way a child *can* learn. It is appropriate to childness, as a child's body is appropriate to childness.

An adult is not a child.

With that fact come both advantages and disadvantages. An adult has a greater ability than a child to abstract, to reason, to use words, to question, and to explain. This ability is often used inappropriately. *Thinking-about* can interfere with the simple *doing;* and words can build barriers of misunderstanding. Logic owns a monkey-wrench factory. Adult capabilities can also be used appropriately in learning. Abstraction can distill to essences and words can build bridges as well as walls.

We must, therefore, be careful in our enthusiasm for learning like a child to avoid throwing the adult out with the bathwater. Monkey-see-monkey-do is the first and simplest school, but if the price of readmission for the adult is his *consciousness of learning,* then the price is too great.

The parent who looks at a Picasso drawing and announces he has a 4-year-old at home who can "do that," may be nearly right—if what he means is the *drawing.* But the drawing on the wall isn't the work of art; it is only symbolic of it. The work of art is the adult consciousness that produced the childlikeness in the drawing.

Dancer/choreographer Twyla Tharp moves with the nonchalance and apparent aimlessness of a 4-year-old, but the artistry in her movement is the adult consciousness behind it. That's what catches the throat; not only the artlessness, but the artlessness in the art.

Adults can best concern themselves, then, not in learning *like* a child, but in learning *from* a child. No adult wants to ski the way a child skis, but rather with a child's spirit—with the same totalness of experience and immediacy in the doing, unencumbered by the inappropriate. We do not need to deny our adult consciousness for that.

What we need, rather, is to become aware of the pulsating two-sidedness of our learning process, and go with the beat. We need to hearken to the rhythm of the *whole* and the *parts,* of the *general* and the *specific,* balancing the reasoning faculty of our left brain and the intuitive nature of our right brain. Each hemisphere does what it does best—analyzes or synthesizes—*not in opposition, but in concert.* One side of the brain provides one view, the other side another view, and there—where the images overlap—a new figure emerges in focus, deeply dimensional, even hologrammic. And that is learning.

LIES YOUR BODY TELLS YOU

In learning motor skills some people are more *physically literate* than others. When they see someone do something, whether it's a dance step or a kick turn, they *read* the action correctly and imitate it. Sometimes they get only the general feel of the movement at first, the outline. "Hey, do that again." Receptive of body and mind, they appear to be imprinted with the movement and replicate it.

If they produce the movement only generally on the first attempt, they then check the image of it in their head—matching their sensing of their bodies against that image. Or they check the reality of the model, seeking specific answers. Let's see, does the right hand pass over the head or to one side? Does the left leg step directly to the front, or obliquely? The kinesthetic echo of the image reverberates throughout their body. Back and forth they go from the specific to the general, the parts to the whole, relating, differentiating, and adjusting. They are learning.

Others simply do not have that facility. Some people apparently can neither *sense* nor *see* what is being done in an action. There is no kinesthetic empathy in response to the movement. They have neither an overall sense of the larger movement nor an eye for its details. Although innate differences in physical literacy range over a wide scale, many people simply do not use what they have. They have blocked or subverted their natural ability to imitate movement with their habitual tensions or an overriding intellection. The physical aspects of their experiencing have been slighted in preference for the intellectual or emotional aspects. They are out of balance. They *think about* or *worry about* instead of simply *moving.*

Some people see the action clearly. They can describe it; they can tell whether or not another person is doing it "right," but they cannot—or will not—do it themselves. There is a breakdown in their internal communication system. They are perhaps of the opinion, that their knees are bent when they are not bent. They think that their hands are forward when they are not forward. Ski instructors, usually glib physical literates themselves, are often baffled by such people. "Bend the knees," they tell them; the rigid knees remain. "Do this," they say, bending their knees; the pupils smile, confident that the instructor can't mean *them* because they are already *doing this*. Except that they are not. The messages from their muscles and tendons are being misprojected into an image of what their body looks like and what it is doing that bears little resemblance to what their body *actually* looks like, or what it is actually doing.

Fortunately, practice can help in both instances: kinesthetic awareness can be enhanced and the body image can be corrected.

"You can observe a lot by just watching," Yogi Berra said. He has a point. *Watch* all moving things—people, animals, the trees in the wind. Sense the whole movement, getting the feel of it; then look to the details. Notice how people walk, run, sit, and stand. What's the overall feel of the movement? Then notice the details; where do the knees go, what part of the foot touches ground first, how much do the arms swing, which way do the palms face, is one shoulder higher than another? Sense the relationship between the moving parts, how apparent causes and effects spiral through the body to produce the whole. If tiny lights were placed on every joint, what pattern would they trace on a time-exposure photograph?

When you have seen with your eyes, then see with your body. Imitate the animals, the trees in the wind, and the people. (Use your judgment and sense of self-preservation as to where and when you do this.) Get their *look* into your body and translate it into a specific feeling or sensation. Sometimes, when you strike accurately upon someone's unique way of doing you'll feel that you *feel* like that person, as if you've captured their essence, their very way of being, as well as their way of doing.

On the ski slope watch other skiers—experienced skiers, and novice skiers—not to compare or judge or note intellectually what they "should" be doing, but just to see what they *are* doing, and how the doings relate. Notice that the waving right arm is more than a waving arm; it is also a displaced hip or an inappropriately straight leg. Nothing happens in isolation; notice that, and trace the intricacies of the connections. Then put those intricacies into your own body; try them on and notice what happens, how you feel and what you sense.

This role-playing is not to find a skiing style that appeals to you enough to copy and wear as your own; it is to understand more clearly how *feelings* and *appearances* relate and how their dynamics interplay. By trying on a skier's technique you get a flavor of the *feeling* behind it; then you notice how that feeling resonates in you, courses through your body, and expresses itself in your skiing. Because you are different, the *look* of the skiing will be different, even though the inspiration is a similar *feeling*.

The way to ski more like Jean-Claude Killy, therefore, is not to win a Killy ski-alike contest, but to allow your skiing to express your individual experience as much as Killy's skiing is an expression of his experience. The most perfect copy of an original cannot capture what made the original worth copying. The sharpest knife cannot cut itself.

As well as practicing your observation of others, practice developing an accurate body image—a picture of your body in space as it *is*, not as you think it is or wish it were. That will mean tuning into sensations dulled by your ignoring them, and becoming aware of existing tensions, even though you believe yourself to be relaxed. It may mean, too, discovering that the body is a liar.

In the workshops, to demonstrate the perfidy of the body and the falseness of its feedback, I use a simple exercise you can try right now.

With your eyes closed, stand (or sit) with your arms level, outstretched straight in front of you. Raise your right arm at about a 45° angle and lower the left hand a comparable amount. Hold that position for 10 or 20 seconds, eyes still closed. Then bring your arms back to level again. Open your eyes and check the results.

Try it now.

Ordinarily there is a discrepancy between what the body *feels* is level and what the eyes *see* as clearly not level. The right arm is almost always higher than the left by several inches.

Sometimes, when I give this exercise to a group, there are one or two people who seem pleased with themselves for getting it *right,* that is, coming out level. But *right* is *wrong.* Although I make no claims to scientific sampling, in my experience with giving the exercise to t'ai chi classes and skiing, golf, and tennis workshops, I have found that the students who end up with level arms are usually less physically literate—less able to imitate an action correctly—than the others.

The highly physically literate workshop instructors—John,

Peter, Martin, and Bucky—even though they have been through it dozens of times, have yet to come out anywhere near level. And Sigi, who admits to "cheating" by consciously compensating for the discrepancy he now knows will be there, still ends up every time with a wide gap between his arms.

The reason there is a gap, if reason you must have, has to do with stretch reflexes in the muscles, but I give the exercise strictly for its shock effect. It jolts the unquestioned faith the students have in their body images; it demonstrates to them that what *feels* right may not *be* right. That is an important first step in breaking any unsupported reliance on a *feeling of rightness* the skiers might have. Seat-of-the-pants flyers similarly must learn to doubt their kinesthetic judgments if they are going to learn to trust their instruments in IFR conditions.

When the skiers understand that any of their faulty habits, imposed on their bodies by long misuse, have the sanctity of *rightness* through familiarity alone, they are more receptive to change. The idea is to transfer temporarily to an exterior source the criteria for rightness (rightness in the sense of aptness to the task and appropriateness). The body is then led into more appropriate movements until these movements begin to feel equally *right*—that is, until the new ways are as familiar as the old response. Gradually the new *right* response replaces the old one, which now begins to feel *wrong*.

Voila! Learning has happened.

In the Centered Skiing workshops the temporary exterior sources are (1) the instructors and (2) the videotape system.

• The instructors direct and guide their skiers to an awareness of what the students are *doing,* and to what would be more appropriate to do under the circumstances. Ideally, this is not done in a hortatory do-this-do-that manner, but with a subtle direction of the skier's own awareness, allowing him to discover for himself the new, more appropriate movements.

The instructors also provide a model to imitate. In the workshops we use a technique we call Imprint Skiing in which the pupils follow an instructor down the slope as closely as possible. (This might sound like the venerable "Follow me!" common to every ski school, but we have a scientific anecdote to go with it, and charge more for it.) We tell the skiers about the experiments at Harvard in which impressionable-age ducklings learned to follow a basketball around under the impression that it was their mother. "If a duck can think a basketball is its mother, you can think Peter is yours. Follow him. Imprint!"

• The video machine is a singularly effective smasher of faulty body images. (*If* the skier's ability to "observe by watching" is developed.) It is difficult to support your insistence that you have shed your up-and-down excess when the video replay shows you hiccupping down the slope. It is equally hard to maintain that your downhill knee *is* bent when moving pictures reveal it to be as straight as a ski pole.

With the use of videotape, skiers can learn to match the *objective* image with their *subjective* kinesthetic feeling. For example, a common fault of intermediate skiers is their conviction

that their weight is on their downhill ski when, in fact, it is not — it is predominantly on their uphill ski.

How has this discrepancy between conviction and fact come about? The skiers have misinterpreted the *feeling* and hooked it up in their body computers with the wrong *image*. They feel resistance from their downhill ski and assume that the resistance is evidence that their weight is on that ski. That's how they image themselves, then, with a weighted downhill ski.

The videotape disabuses them of that image. It shows a skier with a rigid downhill leg (either straight or with a knee frozen in a fixed bent position) braced against the downward slope of the mountain. This action displaces all the skier's weight onto the uphill ski. The skiers have mistaken the *resistance* they feel as their *weight*; in fact, it is *tension* they feel and the *displacement* of weight.

Aha! The next turn on the slope, when the instructor asks them what they felt in their downhill leg, they will feed the feeling of *resistance* (if that is what they felt) to their computers and come up with the image of a *rigid leg*. No longer will they match that feeling of resistance with the image of weight-bearing leg; the videotape has corrected their programming.

However, the *right* feeling when weight is actually on the downhill ski—a yielding, forward-moving flow—will not necessarily *feel* right immediately. It will be strange, and it is apt to feel strange. But gradually, through use and attended awareness, the new feeling will hook up with the right image—the feel of the bending, yielding knee and the sight of the smooth turn seen in the tape.

The skier may from time to time return to that old feeling of resistance in his downhill leg that was *home* for so long, but now the inner image, having been rematched by the video experience, will recognize the feeling for what it is—an old address.

Instructors sometimes say, when a pupil has done something right for the first time, "Hey, terrific! How did that feel?" Pupils usually answer, "Good!" because they are as eager to say the right thing as to do the right thing. It is possible that what felt *good* was the instructor's praise rather than their new way of doing.

Anyway, it would be more useful to investigate, instead of *how* it felt, *where* it felt—in the knees, in the feet, in the hips—and *what* was felt, or better yet, *sensed*. Workshop instructors use the word *sense* rather than *feel* because of the variety of meanings *feel* has. "How did that feel?" is often taken as a request for a value judgment rather than the exploration of an experience. And thus the pupil comes up with "good." Time would be better spent searching out a metaphor to illuminate the feeling rather than characterizing it. "It felt as if my knee was melting and dripping hot tallow into my boot" is of more value in learning than "it felt good."

THE CAMEL'S SECRET

"Camel's Hump" is the name of a mountain near where I live in Vermont. "Hogback" is the name of another mountain in the southern part of the state—and doubtless in many other states, too. Wherever mountains loom and men name them there are metaphors—the drawing on some similarity in the experiencing of two quite different things, and the commenting on the commonality with a name.

The world is metaphor. Queen Anne's lace, jack-in-the-pulpit, buttercup, cattail. *What's it like?* Well, it's like a swallow's tail...a bear's tooth...a haystack...a dog's hind leg.... Thus do we fence with familiarity that which is alien and different. With the feeling of familiarity comes the feeling of understanding.

"A mind free to respond cannot help doing two things to whatever confronts it: it *connects and it animates.*" Poet Stanley Burnshaw says in his book *The Seamless Web.* *

Connects and animates: The similarities in dissimilars are connected; their new relationship animates them with meaning. The unknown of one is explained in the known terms of the other. Strangers meet and, discovering they have a common relative, learn something about each other and themselves. That is metaphor.

Hold your ski poles as if you had a Hershey bar in each hand. You don't want to drop them, but you don't want to melt them, either.

Your knees are elbow macaroni. Now cook them.

In the turn, your head is the bubble in a carpenter's level on your shoulders. Keep it centered.

The mountain is a dish of vanilla ice cream and you are hot fudge. Flow your way down the slope.

---

*[Italics added] Also from the book: "A metaphor is what happens when one looks in a certain way, just as a sneeze is what happens when one looks at the sun."

It is all nonsense to some, but for others in that nonsense there is a spark that arcs from hemisphere to hemisphere in their brain. The metaphor is verbal and resonates in the left hemisphere with words; the metaphor is imagery and resonates in the right hemisphere with pictures. They join, relate, and communicate with the entire organism. "I see!" says the verbal side. *Aha* flashes its silent lightning across the landscape of the image side. There is a joining, and learning happens.

It is difficult to teach a motor skill by telling someone what to *do*, because the thing that must be *done* is a *feeling*, a kinesthetic, wholly, subjective sensation. To teach, then, something must be said (or done) that communicates the necessary *feeling* or sensation.

The exquisite Balinese dancers are, from the times they are tiny children, taught by physical manipulation. Silently, teachers guide the youngsters' hands and body, shaping them into the correct postures, until the children absorb the *feeling* of the movements into their bodies.

Another way to communicate the feeling of a movement is to relate to it other familiar movements and other actions. Metaphor, whether verbal or visual, is a direct way to do this.

Billy Brauer, my artist friend who did the cover and the drawings for this book, is a golfer. He told me about a pro who was seriously off his game, and was sitting dejectedly in the clubhouse after yet another disastrous round. The pro was approached by another pro, a sympathetic and knowing friend, who said nothing but simply chucked a book of matches at him in a sidearm motion as if skipping a rock. *Enlightment,* just as in the Zen stories. In the metaphor of the matchbook toss, the golfer realized what had been missing from his swing. It was that same under-and-through *whipping feeling* in his right hand. Connects and animates, indeed.

I was in a weekend golf workshop given by Gene Coghill and L.V. Brown for Esalen Institute in which a carpet was draped over a wire and whacked at with an old-fashioned carpet beater in a metaphor for the golf swing. They wanted to show that the body, the physical being, knew perfectly well how to *swing;* it was the emotional complexities of swinging *at a golf ball* that caused trouble. As long as the participants were ignorant of the lesson's intent, they made perfect swinging motions at the rug. Gradually some began catching on and *aha* happened. But one, when he saw what Coghill and Brown were getting at, started swinging at the carpet much the same way he attacked golf balls—tensely, fiercely, and ineffectually. Coghill remarked, "Your pursuit of golf has damaged your carpet beating."

What connects and animates is a highly individual matter. A metaphor that is *aha* for one is *huh* for another; yet we tend to treat the metaphor that works for *us* as universal, *the* secret, the talisman for all time. In my years of taking lessons in everything from welding to fly-casting, I have been taught by teachers who treated their favorite metaphor as if it had been passed to them on a stone tablet. Since it was the vehicle of their personal delivery, they constantly repeat it with the only variation an increase in decibels.

If you are a student of such one-talisman teachers you will be best served by falling back on your own devices. Use your left-brained logic to figure out intellectually exactly what point the instructor is trying to make, then search your own experience to come up with a metaphor that makes a connection and animates the point for you.

"Oh, I see, you mean sort of *melt* the downhill knee!" (Perhaps not high on the *satori* meter, but if it works, it works.)

The next time that instructor's pet metaphor draws a blank, he brightens: "Sort of *melt* your downhill knee!"

"Whaddya mean, melt?"

"Well, you know, *melt*—what does it mean to you?"

"Messy and gooey and running all over the place." To each his own metaphor.

Instructors in search of a metaphor that connects and animates should consider the backgrounds of their individual students. What are their interests? Where in their stream of experience can a bridge best be built? I once helped a woman overcome a disconcerting driving habit that involved consistently clipping curbs with the rear wheel while making right turns. I simply reminded her of the well-known Vacuum Cleaner Effect. Anyone who has ever pulled a cannister vacuum cleaner from room to room—and she had—knows you have to take a wide enough line to keep the thing from hanging up on the doorjamb. "Aha!" she exclaimed. And she has added miles to the life of her tires.

I helped my inexperienced co-driver, a musician, learn the long and complicated Nürburgring course in Germany by breaking it into movements for him—a successful metaphor, even though during the race he crashed my Ferrari in adagio.

In this "universe which thinks and feels by likenesses" (Burnshaw again) I cannot imagine either teaching or learning without metaphor. Yet in the metaphor's importance lurks a danger: the danger of *hanging on* to metaphor, of *getting stuck* on it. Once you have the *feeling*, let go of the metaphor. As Chuang Tzu said, once you have netted the fish, forget the net; once you have snared the rabbit, forget the snare. The metaphor is the finger pointing to the moon, not the moon. Use it accordingly.

Consider the secrets you have gleaned from time to time while learning a sport, the few words from a pro that connected and illuminated, sending you home grinning with "I've got it!" Then the secret stopped working; you lost it. But you got another one. "This is really it this time. I've got it!" And it, too, failed after a while, wore out, and lost its magic. Those were false secrets, you decide, fool's gold, and you continue your search for the real secret, the end-all secret.

They are not false at all. The metaphors and the secrets that worked and then ceased to work did not let you down; they are no less The Secret now than they once were. If anything you let *them* down; you caught them in free flight and tried to fix their wings in plastic. Let go.

And anyway, the secret of skiing *isn't secret.*

10

CONCENTRATING

This is what intelligence is; paying attention to the right things. **—EDWARD T. HALL**

During my childhood summers spent in Colorado, our water supply ran by the door as Willow Creek, a stream that polished speckled stones and harbored speckled trout and glinted in its narrow banks. Standing on a footbridge without rails I played games with the creek. Sighting down between my toes I bade the water cease its flow and the bridge, instead, to move upstream.

It did.

Then I commanded the bridge to stand still and the water to flow again. It did. Quickly now; flow, stop. It was a fine way to get to that dizzy state much honored by children.

I didn't know it, but I was playing games with *figure/ground*—a term from Gestalt psychology. The *ground*, or background, is the setting, the context against which the *figure* is the focus of interest. I was rapidly changing figure and ground, with the constant of motion appearing to belong first to the stream and then to the bridge.

In the same way we see optical illusions first one way and then another. The one reproduced on these pages is probably the best known. Look at it with the white as the ground, and two black profiles emerge facing each other. Look at it with the black as a ground, and the figure of a white vase appears. Then bid one to be; and then the other. Slowly at first, then faster. It is a tongue twister for the eyes.

Some experts say you can "see" the drawing only one way at a time; either you see the vase or you see the faces, but you cannot see both at once. I disagree, but it doesn't matter whether you can see both at once, or not. What matters is, once you have

seen both vase and faces, once you are aware of their relationship, there is yet a third way of looking at the drawing: with the *knowledge* that whatever you see, there is a different way of seeing it. While seeing the faces you are aware the vase exists; while seeing the vase you are aware the faces are yours for a simple flick of attention. This awareness changes the seeing.

In learning something like skiing, flexibility in playing with figure and ground is essential. It is necessary to flick in and out, back and forth, from part to whole, from specific to general. Although your attention is on the one aspect, you never lose awareness of its relationship to the other. You are never out of touch with the totality, the unity of the aspects.

As you concentrate on your pole plant, for instance, or on your edge set, or your weight transfer, you also carry an awareness of how that part fits into the whole of the turn. And how that turn relates to these parts. Back and forth—easily, quickly—parts and wholes, until they are experienced as one. There is the *figure;* there is the *ground;* there is the *totality* of the one experience.

Then, what *needs* attention *draws* attention, naturally and surely. Getting *stuck* is losing that flexibility, that free interplay of figure and ground, and that leads to the trouble known as loss of concentration.

DISTRACTION AS ATTRACTION

Concentration, like relaxation, flees pursuit. Yet we tend, in our world, to regard concentration as something imposed on ourselves, something requiring effort, something we *make* ourselves do. But concentration is an *attraction,* a drawing of our attention.

We tend to think of concentration as a *narrowing* of focus, a deliberate limiting of experience, like putting blinkers on a horse. But concentration comes in many "widths." Though it is capable of fine selectivity, it should not be limiting.

We tend to mistake such things as *worrying about* or *thinking about* for concentration. (Am I doing this right? Am I going too fast? Is this the way it's supposed to feel?) That is not concentration. Indeed, it represents a disturbance in concentration—burbles and eddies in the smooth flow of attention.

Concentration is a flexible awareness of what is important and what is not important to the task-of-the-moment. It is a clear differentiation between which is *figure* and which is *ground.* It is attending to the figure while being aware of the ground.

Failures in concentration represent a disturbance in the interplay of figure and ground. Instead of attention, concern, interest, attraction, fascination, there is tension, confusion, diffusion, compulsion, fixation, anxiety, self-consciousness, boredom.

Take Ilie Nastase for an example. He is notorious for the fickleness of his concentration despite his prodigious talents as a tennis player. When a match is going well for him there is no question that the immediate court situation—this point, this ball—is a clear *figure* to which he attends. He is concentrating.

But let something go awry, a dubious line call perhaps, and you see before your eyes the rapid disintegration of that concentration. Figure and ground are scrambled like so many breakfast eggs. Suddenly the sideline photographers, whose motorized Nikons have not intruded on his consciousness before, are the focus of the Nastase ire. They are too noisy; they tease his peripheral vision. The photographers have emerged as *figure,* although they have nothing to do with the task at hand. Nastase's attention has been snagged on them, and his concentration is in shards. He is driven to complaints, to mischief, to delays and is sadly, perplexedly incapable of collecting his fragmented energies and returning to his game with any direction. He is a cork upon the sea.

Another athlete of superior talents whose problems with concentration have been discussed in the national press is Bert Blyleven, a pitcher with the Texas Rangers.* For him, a distinguishing feature of concentration is: "When you lose it you don't know you've lost it." Until, perhaps, the sound of bat on ball jolts him back to awareness.

Typically, Blyleven would be distracted by something—a strangeness in the feel of the resin bag, for instance. His mind would hook on that, wondering why it felt so odd, while the rest of him went on automatic pilot and continued pitching—until that crack of the bat.

The mind is a drunken monkey, the yogis say, and it certainly plays the part—reeling from one matter of rapidly exhaustible interest to another. Anyone who has sought a stilling of the mind through meditation of one form or another knows the difficulties in shutting off an incessant chatter in the head, or in attending to one single thought without being visited by an unbidden swarm of others. At first it is surprisingly difficult to attend only to a mantra, a mandala, a candle flame, or for that matter to a 5.2-mile racecourse in the ninth hour of a 12-hour motor race. Or, to a batter with a two-and-two count, two out and one on in the first. The monkey meanders off.

When attention wanders it is not that you have *lost* concentration, so much as you have lost what you were "supposed" to be concentrating on. You are now attending to something quite different from what you intended. You have been distracted. But a *dis*traction is merely an *at*traction elsewhere. A new, more compelling *figure* has emerged from the background and drawn your attention to it.

Sports Illustrated, June 14, 1976. "The Stuff and No Nonsense" by Pat Jordon.

The new attraction is called a *dis*traction because it is irrelevant to the task-of-the-moment, to what you "should" be concentrating on. You should be concentrating on the capitols of the Western states, not on the woodpecker outside the window. You should be concentrating on keeping this pitch low and inside, or on the brake point for the hairpin turn, or on counting your inhalations.

In many cases you are surrounded by a concert of commonly shared *shoulds* with which you are out of tune; you do not share the figure the others have agreed is important: this batter, this point, this problem on the blackboard. The figure that has your attention may not be relevant to the other people or to the task, but it *is* relevant to you, or you would not be drawn to it. For you, now, it's the right thing to pay attention to, as inappropriate as it might be for what is supposed to command your interest. *You cannot be distracted without your own complicity.*

If you hearken to the shoulds around you and *make* yourself concentrate, you are engaging in a battle wasteful of energy. You have, first, the energy directed to *doing* the task; then the energy *resisting* the effort to do the task; and, finally, the energy directed at *fighting the resistance.* All this energy and resistance is yours. You have fielded both teams as well as the referee. Exhausting.

It is more efficient and effective if, instead of *compelling* your attention to a task, you allow your attention to *be attracted* to it. In this approach to concentration is the difference between a star and a planet, between an object shining with its own light or merely reflecting the light from a beam directed at it.

In tennis, the advice to "keep your eye on the ball," is a light from *outside,* a forced attention. "Find something interesting in the ball," is putting a light *inside.* Tennis pros who tell their students to notice the patterns the seams make or to look for the brand name as the ball comes to them are suggesting ways of *drawing* the eye to the ball rather than *forcing* it there.

In skiing, when an instructor tells you to concentrate on something such as your pole plant or your knees, translate that to mean *find something of interest* there. It is up to you to discover something that will attract your interest—the particular pressure of your boot on your shin when your knees bend, the gloved fist in the corner of your eye as your pole is planted. Find the *feel* of it—a sensation or an image—to notice. You can stay with a sensation more easily than you can with a thought. The physical is here/now while the drunken mental monkey leaps to past and future, dragging in anxieties and ought-to's, and muddying the simplicity of the doing.

Blyleven, the pitcher, is quite right—recognizing that you've lost your concentration is not easy. Sometimes it has simply wandered off, not attaching itself to anything of any particular strength. No strong figure has attracted it; it has simply gone walkabout over a dull landscape.

Sometimes, however, a new figure emerges abruptly to grab the attention. This condition is harder than bored inattention to recognize as a "loss" of concentration. Your internal checkers continue to register the intensity of your involvement but cannot tell that the object of your attention has changed. Blyleven may still be *concentrating,* but he is concentrating on the odd feel of the resin bag and not on his next pitch.

This kind of concentration loss, in which a new competing figure has broken the desired attachment, is best dealt with by *attending to* the new figure—going where it leads until its ability to command your attention has faded. Follow it. Give it your full attention and your interest will be quickly sated; deny its obvious interest to you and it will continue to pull your sleeve at the edge of your awareness. It is the *unfinished business* in such a figure that keeps it from receding into the background and allowing you to get back fully to the task-of-the-moment.

There is the classic story: Two monks were traveling a road together that was crossed by a flood-engorged stream. A beautiful young woman stood in the path asking for assistance in crossing. The first monk, eyes straight ahead, slipped past her and plunged on. The second monk lifted her in his arms, carried her across the stream, and set her on the opposite bank. Several miles farther along the path, the first monk turned on the second, "How could you do that? How could you forget your vows so quickly and touch that woman?" The second monk said, "Oh, are you still carrying her? I put her down long ago."

Attend, then, to your own resin bag or your own young woman by the stream. Adjust the boot that nags you, fix the pole strap, replace your scratched goggles. Or decide that they will not be bothersome after all, and let them recede from your attention. Deal with the niggling distractions one way or another and empty them of interest for you.

This technique of eliminating disruptive new figures by

granting them temporary but total attention is not suitable for all circumstances. In my experience in motor racing I found that giving total attention, for instance, to a puzzling pit signal your crew has just flashed to you can find you suddenly deeper in the next turn than prudence dictates. (Of course, there is nothing like a shot of adrenalin to return you to the here/now.)

When I was racing, the general wisdom was that your concentration was safe if your mind was on anything that dealt immediately with your race—on anything that moved along *with* you, or was coming up *ahead* of you. I learned to let drop any interest in what was stationary as soon as I passed it. I learned to evaluate quickly the relevance of an emerging figure and rank it accordingly. The hook of a confusing pit signal was, therefore, best let go immediately, and the energy surge from its confusion directed to being doubly alert to what was traveling in my immediate space—my instruments, my tires, or my road companions who might be gaining on me or being gained on by me.

When there is an on-going activity that *must* be attended to, it is better to keep a constant running check on the state of your concentration. It is better to maintain your attentiveness at a steady state in which any deviation from the norm stands out sharply and can be instantly rated for importance. In racing and in flying, you can use a patterned scan of your instruments and the exterior world as it is represented in your windshield or rearview mirrors. Your immediate environment is kept in an even wash of awareness. Your attention creates a smooth, bland field against which the smallest changes emerge immediately as a powerful figure—a change in angle of an instrument's needle, for instance, or the appearance of a speck in the upper right quadrant of a plane's windshield. The emergent figure is evaluated and ordered for priority, and the scan goes on.

Patterns and rituals, designed to weave just such a neutral field, are common to many other activities and vary from individual to individual. They often surface as superstitions—lucky shirts or lucky colors or lucky breakfast menus, for instance. In sports, these patterns are particularly important for those who *act* rather than *react*—the bowler, the pitcher in baseball, the server in tennis, the player at the free-throw line in basketball, and, perhaps most of all, the golfer. It is no happenstance that golfers are the largest market for gadgets, gimmicks, tricks, and secrets, the better to ply their sport.

The best golfers have evolved specific systems or techniques for collecting their concentration and Centering their energies. They have established patterns of addressing the ball, waggling the club, looking at certain spots a certain number of times. Everything they do is aimed at keeping themselves free from inappropriate tensions which will interfere with the delicate balance between *causing* and *allowing.*

As a skier, you, too, seek that balance between causing and allowing. It is similarly helpful for you to have certain checks for your awareness, your concentration, to allow tension to be reclaimed as useful energy.

Open your awareness, first, with attention to your breathing, noticing it, allowing it its fullness. Follow it to your Center, then let it widen your receptivity to the sensations in the world around you and within you. Follow it to the extremities of your body, to your hands in your gloves, your toes in your boots, and the roots of your hair.

Feel the beat of your heart and the course of your blood. Hear the cicada sounds of your silence in your ears.

Feel yourself as mass and form with boundaries but no barriers. Relate your mass and form to the masses and forms around you. Relate your energies to the energies around you — to the mountain, the sun, the woods, the people. Be where you are. This is concentration.

Do not make the mistake of *narrowing* your focus before you have *broadened* your range of being. Open yourself to the widest field of awareness possible, without preconceived notions and barriers; then allow specific figures to emerge, free of compulsion.

Concentration, Charlotte Selver says, is con-cent-tration, "coming to a mutual center."

The human consciousness can be conscious of its consciousness, aware of what it is aware of, and aware of the awareness at the same time: dimension on dimension. Some spend lifetimes in adding to that chain of awareness, holding the image of the image of the image — like mirrors reflecting mirrors reflecting mirrors — and using no more effort than a mirror makes in reflecting an image, or an image makes in being reflected. In such a state there can be no *dis*traction because everything is equally attended to, everything is an equal attraction. Figure/ground are unified and bathed in one perfect light. But don't count on reaching that space before the next NASTAR race.

You can, however, improve your concentration before then by *letting up on your efforts to improve it.* Allow it more leeway to permit it more flexibility in the interplay of figure and ground. "If we are more lenient with ourselves," Fritz Perls, father of Gestalt therapy, said, "we are more likely to work up an efficient interest in the task."

Concentration is nothing more than the relaxed/alert state mentioned throughout this book. It is a relaxed widening of awareness with an alert responsiveness to changes.

LET IT BE, LET IT BE

It is not easy for a people steeped in a culture that stitches samplers of Try, Try Again and gives A's for Effort to accept the idea that the struggle is often best won by *letting go.*

"That's a dangerous thing to say around a kid," a workshop skier says. Like many others he equates letting go with *giving up* — quitting — that grim specter that haunts the benches from Little League to the pros. But giving up is not the opposite of trying; it is often a result of it. The result of trying hard and failing, even trying hard and *succeeding.* In a goal-oriented society the goal fallen short of or the goal attained that sometimes turns ashen in the mouth can lead equally to *giving up.*

In a life organized around *end-gaining,* success can be as limiting as failure. Mark Spitz won what he set out to win in the Munich Olympics, but since then has seemed to drift. His name has been used to sell several products, but he is best known as a butt of talk-show jokes, and he is Exhibit A for other Olympic heroes on how not to conduct their post-Olympic career, as unfair as that may be. Stan Smith accomplished his goal of winning at Wimbledon, and then his game mysteriously fell apart. He has been years getting it back together again. Chris Evert is wiser than either. When reporters ask her, "What are your goals now?" she answers, "I have no specific goals." What she is saying is, "I refuse to limit myself." And you can hardly call Chris Evert unmotivated.

Letting go is letting go of the attachment to specific goals — seven gold medals, the championship, making the team, breaking the record — and attending to the path. The path might lead *through* seven gold medals, the club championship, making the team, breaking the record, but it does not *end* there abruptly, leaving you to say, "Is this all there is? I thought it would be different...."

Letting go is *means* oriented; it is playing the process, not the result. It is being where you are at the time you are there. It is recognizing that getting there is not only half the fun, it is all there is. "If you have something, give it up," F.M. Alexander said. "*Getting* it, not *having* it, is what you want."

Paradoxically, *letting go* of trying can be more successful than trying. Don't *try* to do something, simply do it.

Perhaps Roger Bannister tried many times to break the 4-minute mile, but on the day he succeeded he didn't *try* to do it, he did it. If that is puzzling, do this experiment. *Try* to lift your right hand. Did you do it? Then you didn't *try* to lift it, you lifted it. Try again. This time did you *not* lift your right hand? Well, then, you can clearly see which was the more successful—doing it or trying to do it.

Don't misunderstand; actually *doing* something, whether lifting your right hand or winning a race, is not without *effort*. You could not watch the tapes of Franz Klammer's thrilling downhill performance at Innsbruck without being struck by the effort involved, but it was a perfect matching of effort to task. It hovered, at throat-catching times, on the brink of a mismatch.

Too often, *trying* bespeaks excessive effort, an attempt to overwhelm, and often such trying falls on the other side of the *doing*. Less would have hit the mark. Less would have been more.

DON'T MAKE IT HAPPEN

I studied acting one year long ago with Sanford Meisner in his evening classes at the Neighborhood Playhouse in New York. Like the study of Chinese, it helped my skiing; that's where I first heard the phrase: *Don't make it happen, let it happen.*

In class we worked in pairs improvising scenes in which we discovered usable truths about ourselves— our *selves* being our only "instrument" in acting. We learned what triggered what responses in those selves, thus mapping our emotions so we would have known paths when a future script called for particular responses. The idea is that you fill out the scripted emotions with the reality of your own experience, and thus make the experience real for the audience. (However, I never got that far. I never got beyond improvisations and a few scenes because my daytime career as a journalist was leading into interesting areas.)

In the improvisations, a pair of us would put ourselves in a situation, establish a conflict, and then, ideally, react to it with honesty. "Don't make it happen, let it happen," Sandy said. Nothing happened however hard I tried.

I remember clearly, some 20 years later, the evening of the dawning. It is not that I did anything differently, it was that I *did* nothing. I was simply there, and it turned out that was the place I had been looking for so fiercely. Just as a stereopticon slides into focus, there was an effortless sliding into place of a wider, clearer, very *present,* more dimensional world. Blinders fell away; there was a lightness, a clarity, a playful spontaneity. And things *happened,* really happened. How I threw things and carried on! But it grew out of the reality of the moment, not out of a plan in my head.

"Don't make it happen, let it happen." Why didn't you say it was so *easy!*

That's what wrong with letting it happen, of course—it is *ease-y,* effortless, and we do not trust the effortless way. We seem to have absorbed through our very pores the notion that there is some unnamed merit in the hard way. We credit as "real" only that which we *do on purpose,* that which takes teeth-gritting effort. We belittle or ignore that which we do without deliberate intention, that which seems to *happen.* If we cannot take credit for the doing, we discredit it.

In one of our skiing workshops there was a pleasant young physicist whose skiing was larded with eager excess. Somehow he was inveigled into doing something on skis that stripped away that effort and left only ease and simplicity and fine skiing. It was perfect. But rather than being pleased he seemed bewildered and somehow cheated that it was not harder to do, now that he'd done it. His sense of agentry, his role as the *doer,* had been usurped. He had been robbed of his sense of achievement.

One could guess that he did not want to *lose* his faults so much as he wanted to *conquer* them. He seemed to prefer the trying-to-succeed to the success.

A similar reaction was noted by Tim Gallwey in *The Inner Game of Tennis.* At least one of his students, to whom he had taught a less effortful more effective serve, chose to return to his old serve, haphazard as the results were. With his old serve he had a clearer sense of *doing* something rather than having something just *happen.* He wanted the credit, the boost for his ego when his serve was good. He didn't want some mysterious It hitting the ball, however well.

Athletes are not the only ones who sometimes prefer to hang on to their effort and their egos. Among others are some musicians. David Krehbiel, who occupies the first French horn chair of the San Francisco Symphony, has given workshops for his fellow horn players in which he teaches a more relaxed, less effortful way toward playing better. His approach has not met universal favor. Apparently his colleagues, who chose a singularly difficult instrument to play in the first place, still prefer that the answer to that age-old question, "How do you get to Carnegie Hall?" remain: "Practice!" They prefer to suffer for their art, and to tell them that suffering is not necessary, somehow for them diminishes their art.

Apparently, some want the *making* it happen more than they want the *happening*. They want to hang on to the illusion that the part of themselves they call "I" is the doer, the causer, the cue ball. In that chimerical power of the ego lies their gratification.

We need, then, to identify not only with our *doing,* but with our *being* as well. We need to appreciate the positive aspects of *nothing,* to find the doing in the not-doing.

Wu-wei is the Taoist expression for the power of positive not-thinking. It is the action in nonaction, the knowing in not-

knowing, the something in nothing, the doing in not-doing. *Wu-wei* is the strength of a willow in a wind storm, the resistance in yielding. It is *t'ai chi.*

Wu-wei is following the way of water, the way of wind. It is not the absence of action, but it is the absence of *trying.* Wind is never still, but it has no intention. Water ever seeks its own level, but not on purpose.

Wu-wei: The balance point of being and doing.

For me, the idea is best conveyed not by a passage from the *Tao te Ching* or a quote from the Chuang Tzu, but by a common graffito. I have seen several variations of it, all with dubious attributions for the quotations, but the point is unaffected. One version:

"To do is to be" — John Stuart Mill
"To be is to do" — Jean-Paul Sartre
"Do-be-do-be-do" — Frank Sinatra

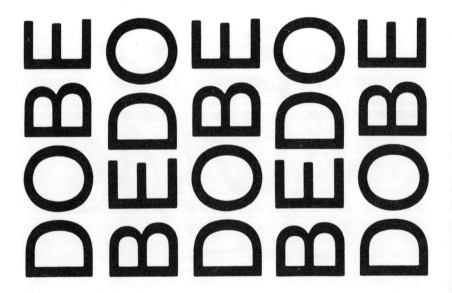

11

THE CARVED TURN

There is no such thing as a right position, but there is a right direction. **— F.M. ALEXANDER**

If you have been flipping through this book to find something, *anything,* that might look as if it dealt with how to ski, you've found it. But don't expect a step-by-step sequence of do-this, do-that, or drawings of positions for you to imitate.

There is none of that here.

The risk is too great that someone might mistake some fleeting moment caught by the pen as a final form. Someone might mistake a space that is merely passed through as a destination.

Al Chung-liang Huang, with whom I study *t'ai chi,* teaches in a fluid, almost formless fashion—much to the despair of those who seek bottles before they have anything to put into them. He once threatened to swipe a sign from a bank teller's station because it so perfectly described what he avoids in his teaching. It said, "Next position please."

Look at the mountainside at a ski resort and see the number of skiers going from one position to another—posing like the pictures in the magazines, then lurching on to the next pose. There is no sense of moving in the movement, no awareness of flow, no idea of space, no soul, no *ch'i*. There is just the hiccupping from pose to pose.

Anthropologist Edward Hall remarks in his book *The Hidden Dimension* about the differences between the concept of space in the Western world and that in the East. The West, he says, sees spaces as empty, as an *absence of things*. The Japanese see spaces as relating to other spaces, as intervals. For this they have a word, *ma*. Their "empty" gardens and "sparse" flower arrangements express this concept.

The idea might well be adapted to skiing. Instead of concentrating on where the *things* are—the arms, the legs, the head—the skier can express *ma* by attending to the relationships of the spaces he is shaping and reshaping as he moves. Not *where* is the arm, but how does the space between the arm and the leg relate to the space between the arm and the head? Attending to the interplay of the spaces will encourage some fluidity in movement and help break that next-position-please habit.

I have chosen to explore the carved turn in some detail, because, for many, it is the ultimate in skiing. One might say the Grand Ultimate, those being the high-flown words that are most often used to translate *t'ai chi*. It is my fantasy that the gently essing curve that cleaves the *t'ai chi t'u*—that half-white half-black circle commonly called the *yin/yang* symbol—was made by the carving edge of a ski.

The carved turn is a perfect meditation.

We refer to the carved turn in the Centered Skiing workshops at Sugarbush as the *C turn,* because it is composed of so many different C's. Look at the string of interlocking C's cascading down the edge of the page (like the symbols we used for mountains when we drew maps in junior high school). Those C's make visible the pattern that the *weighted* ski makes in the flowing linkage of carved turns down a slope.

Look at them. Maybe what came as a revelation to me will appear instantly obvious to you: The turn *starts* in the previous turn and it starts long before you reach the spot where you actually turn. The turn isn't *made* at the edge of the trail where it is seen to *happen,* it is made back there in the finish of the last turn. In those long sweepings arcs that go from one edge of the trail to the other, the turns are actually *made* in the middle of the trail, not at the edge.

Many of the faults of a ski turn grow out of the notion that a turn is *made* where it *happens,* and there is (as the trees at the edge approach) much hurrying to get everything in at the last instant, and a feeling that something must be *done.* So the hip is jerked around, the arms wave about, the shoulder drops—or some other such act of little faith. Yet, as we shall see, all that is needed for a turn to happen is to create the conditions for the turn— and *let* it happen. Trust in the physics, and ye shall be served.

One time, while musing about the golf swing, I came up with a definition that is also applicable to a ski turn. *It is an action in which certain things are caused to happen and certain things are allowed to happen. Faults arise in trying to cause what should be allowed.*

Picture for a moment the zigzag design a sprung paper clip makes. Instead of C's there are straight lines leading into curves. That, I think, is the path most skiers draw down the slope. That was my path before carved turns came into my life. Traverse along the straight part, throw in a turn; traverse, throw in a turn. (Skidding, of course; I knew no other way.) Even with the short traverse in turns that appeared to be linked there was clearly a time in which I was turning, a time when I had stopped turning, and a time when I started turning again.

Not so with the C turn. It is *t'ai chi* in its flow, never a going out without a coming back. The *yin* becomes *yang* like sunrise on a sharp mountain ridge. Who can say when the darkness ends and the light begins? One can only say there is change.

Similarly, in a carved turn *yin* and *yang* become one another, define one another. There is no saying now I am turning, now I am not turning, because it is all a turn even when there is no turning visible. The C turns, too, may be little c's and big C's linked together. Assymetrical. But they are never opened-up paper clips.

The carved turn is a child of modern skiing, dependent on the design of the modern ski—its honed edge and calculated side cut. Ski design is as complex as the design of suspension systems on modern race cars which interplay with new tire designs, just as ski design interplays with the design of boots. And the two deal with many of the same forces.

The *carved turn* is dependent on the ski being set steeply in the snow on its inner edge, and being held there by pressure from the skier, so that the change of direction is effected with a minimum of sideslip. The tails of the skis follow closely in the track of the tips, as if on rails.

The *skidded turn* allows the tails of the skis to make a far wider track in comparison with the tips. The skis slip downhill sideways in a greater proportion to their forward motion. A skidded turn thus uses up more of the hill, finishing lower than a carved turn, as a skidding skier soon discovers in trying to follow directly behind a carving skier.*

In the skidded turn, since the ski presents more side area to the fall line, there is more friction and more drag. As a result the skis are slowed and therein lies the appeal of the skidded turn.

Ski racers *carve* their turns to minimize friction. In a well-carved turn their acceleration is discernible. They like that. That is what racing is about—*speed.*

Most recreational skiers *skid* their turns to avoid acceleration. They want to keep their speed within a comfort range. They like that. For them, that's what recreational skiing is about—*control.*

But skidders delude themselves, or so I believe. I think that the skidded turn promises more control than it delivers. I think that the carved turn offers more control than many suspect.

The C turn is more predictable. The angle of the knees and body and the pressure of the feet on the ski can readily control the radius of the carved turn. You can then choose more accurately than with a skidded turn where your turn will happen and where it will leave you on the slope.

The C turn is more precise. It is like writing with a fine italic pen instead of a Magic Marker. The C turn can draw lines between stones, twigs, icy patches with less risk of catching outside edges—something the broad sweep of the skidded ski is heir to.

The C turn controls speed naturally. To slow down, or avoid picking up unwanted speed, you have only to ride the carve farther and let the laws of physics have their way. In a carved turn the arc you are tracing is a segment of a full circle. Where you choose to leave the arc determines the speed you take with

---

*The terms carved and skidded are probably best thought of as abstractions that do not exist in pure form. I doubt that the purely carved turn, with a wake no wider than the ski's tip, has been made on this earth. But some have come close.

you. Racers get in and get out quickly—short segments, practically straight lines—and thus keep their speed up. But for speed control, think of the C as part of an O. To slow down, stay with the arc longer and, as C more nearly approaches O you are riding your carve slightly uphill and slowing down. You can also ride it to a stop.

Let gravity control your speed both in *crescendo* and *diminuendo*.

In the friction of skidding is entropy.

Go with the energy. Carve.

C IS FOR CAMBER, TOO

There is another important C in the carved turn. The C in the ski itself. More than one, really.

Think of your skis now. See them as you recall them. The image we have of our skis is usually the image as we most often see them—in rows in ski shops or as we carry them from car to lift and back. In your imagination stand your skis in front of you, base to base. From a contact point at the shovel notice that they swell outward to where the bindings are fitted and back again to another contact point at the heels. The swell is, of course, *camber*. Camber is there so that when you stand on your skis they flatten against the snow distributing the weight more or less evenly over the entire length—shovel to tail. That's why the proper ski length for you depends on your weight as well as your height. (Not to mention your taste.)

We are used to seeing skis with this camber. We are used to seeing them flattened, too. What we are not used to seeing— unless we watch carefully for it—is a ski curving the other way, bent like a bow into a reverse arc, pressed by the foot into a smooth curve as if the ski were supported only at both ends. Yet, in a turn, the familiar camber of the ski turns into just such *reverse camber*. Look for it in magazine pictures of ski racers.

That bowed arc in the ski, maintained steadily through a turn, is what does the carving.

Another more subtle arc also comes into play when the ski is on edge and bowed in reverse camber. This is the slight waistline or side camber designed into each ski. Once you've put your ski on edge and pressed it into the reverse camber arc, then the side camber of the ski acts to distribute the turning forces in such a way that your ski will either whip around in a short-radius turn or trace a larger C (the size depends on the ski's design). That's one of the differences between a slalom and a downhill ski.

What is important is that all these arcs are conspiring *to turn your ski.* They are so designed, indeed, that once you've set up the ski—weighted it, edged it and kept your energy flowing through it—it can do naught *but* turn. Let it. Any rococo body additions intended to make *sure* that the turn happens are, at best, superfluous, at worst, interferring.

Sigi, in viewing the videotapes over lunch for workshop skiers, often stops the action and points to the excessive flare of snow at the tails. The flare is evidence of excess, a hip or a heel thrust that has exploded the ski out of its carving track. The skier had not trusted the turn to *be;* he thought he had to *do* something to finish it.

Certain things are *caused* (the weighting, the edging) and certain things are *allowed to happen* (the C shape of the turn).

It is a matter of balance: your balance on the skis, of course, but more than that. The balance of the *yin* and *yang* aspects of the turn—the causing and allowing, the doing and the being. The balancing of the forces of gravity, of torsion, and of flexion. You direct all these forces with minimal effort and minimal movement because you are at the stillpoint, the point of power, the Center.

The carved turn is a system, a flow, an interconnectedness. If its parts are pulled out for analysis, loose wires will be hanging from them. Don't forget to put them back and hook them up again. Here are some parts, pulled out and looked at, as incomplete and misleading in their way as a Mercator projection of the earth's roundness.

• The knees are not bent. They are bend*ing,* maybe with adjustments so minute you do not consciously register them. Your knees must have your constant *permission* to bend—a lot, a little— when the terrain requests a bend. Knees held stiffly bent, like a section of elbow pipe, are no different from straight, rigid knees.

144/ THE CENTERED SKIER

Both impede the flow of *ch'i.* Neither has the ability to absorb shocks; instead the stiffness transmits the shocks to the upper body, magnifying there into inelegant bendings at the middle, that are sometimes violent, sometimes comic, never productive.

• In a carved turn, the knees bend to absorb bumpy terrain in such a way as to avoid flattening the ski, or changing the angle in which the edge is riding in the track it carves. (There's an exercise in a doorway I describe soon that will make that clearer to you.) To ensure that the knees make their piston movements, absorbing the bumps in the proper plane (square with shoulders and hips), you must be standing *over* your skis, Centered, facing the ski tips and avoiding the extremes of that type of body angulation known as the "comma."

• The body in the General Position is relaxed/alert, the arms loosely embracing a ball of energy. The poles are held as if they were live birds — tightly enough to prevent their escape, but not so fiercly as to crush the breath from them.

• The consciousness is in the body's Center. Energy circulates upward from there through the upper body, where the breathing is easy. The shoulders carry no excessive tension. The energy flows downward through the legs to a grounding in the snow. An awareness extends the length of the ski edges, sensing their cutting fineness, their carving capability.

• To initiate the turn, *thought* — not much more — directs the ski tips toward the fall line. The thought — as an image or a suggestion — is manifested in a sensation of pressure in the toes nudging the ski tips in the desired path. There is no effort, nothing shows, but the tips will fall away, yielding to gravity. (Another way to get the ski tips aimed into the fall line is to push the heel of the ski uphill, but Sigi teaches the least effortful way, the way that tunes into gravity.)

• The downhill ski bears most of the weight of the skier at this moment, but that is about to change, subtly.

WITHDRAW YOUR WEIGHT

So much has been written about up-unweighting, down-unweighting, and I have been taught (or at least had instructors who were teaching) both ways. Now I see it as all theory, all intellectual exercise. I ignore it. And ski better for my ignore-ance.

Before I met with Sigi's approach to the carved turn, I had settled on an up-and-down motion in my turning. Rise up as you start the turn—knees nearly extended straight—sink down as you finish the turn. Rise, sink, up, down. And somewhere in there the outside ski in the turn was granted the greatest burden of weight. Up-and-down is a technique still commonly taught, and many good skiers do it. Which is fine if they choose to, but they needn't.

I prefer Sigi's smooth, sinuous, stilled-upper-body style. There is no up-and-down visible. Indeed, up-and-down is not only

superfluous, it can interfere with the carving of a turn. Remember that arc of reverse camber which you have bowed into the snow? *Up-and-down movements cause the pressure holding that arc to fluctuate.* Now it's greater, now it's less. This disturbs the turning forces, constantly altering the radius of the turn. Up-and-down complicates a simple process.

Faced with the video evidence of its uselessness, my expensively acquired up-and-down all but disappeared in one morning of skiing. I was beginning to carve away what was unnecessary from my turn, a step toward carving the turn itself.

Withdraw the weight from your downhill ski. *Weight shift, weight transfer*—all phrases with such a heavy feeling and all sounding as if you pick up something—*oof*—and set it down—*whew.* (No wonder the up-and-down is persistent and excessive effort ubiquitous.) Think of all this in another way. Just as you initiated the turn with the light touch of thought on your toes, let the light touch of thought deal with your weight transfer. Think of it as energy and redirect it, as you would turn a valve and reduce or increase the flow of fluid through a pipe.

• Your weight is on your downhill ski (the *outside* ski of your last turn which will be the *inside* ski in the upcoming turn). *Withdraw* that weight from that ski; do not *shift* it to the other ski. Yes, of course, everything's got to be someplace, and if you withdraw your weight from one ski, it will end up on your other ski where you want it, but with an economy of movement that is somehow missing in a weight *shift.* It's all in the thought.

Try it now. Stand up with your knees flexed as if you were skiing. Sense your weight. First, *shift* it from one foot to the other, noticing how that feels, noticing what happens in your upper body. Now as you stand, *withdraw* your weight from your right foot with no conscious decision to *put* it anywhere. Just let it go where it goes. See if you don't sense a difference in the way your knees respond. Maybe your upper body is more stilled, the movement absorbed in the central section of your body, in your Center. Perhaps not. Play with it. Sense the floor with your feet as if they were hands. Sense the floor with your feet *through* your feet. *Withdraw* your weight from one, then the other.

Do the least you can. Then do less.

•With a simple flexion of the wrist, touch your pole to the snow. You need neither reach far forward nor lift your shoulder and hammer the pole home. You create tension by such excess and thus muddy the stream of energy, and your movements change the dynamic relationships of the body parts.

Poles that are the improper length can lead to disruptive compensations. With poles too long you might raise your shoulder to make sure they clear the snow. Or you might turn your hand, palm upward, and plant your pole with an exaggerated outside-to-inside slant. Poles too short can make you bend at the middle. All these actions, as small and as isolated as they might seem, affect your entire body.

There is no such thing as an isolated movement; everything is connected to everything else. The smallest movement, the slightest tension, reverberates throughout your body in a spiraling wave. A new balance is constantly sought with a compensation here, a compensation there.

And as the compensations spiral through the body they affect the messages sent to the skis: less edge, more edge; weight back, weight forward. You might regard these movements as little movements, meaning nothing, but to the skis, where they meet the snow, these movements are *signals*—just as every little movement of a rider is a signal to a horse trained for dressage. The skis, and the horse, will react to what you are actually *doing,* not to what you think you are doing, or meant to do.

Clarify your signals and eliminate that which is confusing.

• Now change your edges. Your pole plant, the rhythm keeper of your turn, marks the moment to change smoothly and quickly from one edge to the other—from your outside edge where most of your weight is now riding, to the inside edge of your (yet) uphill ski, which will do the carving.*

To change edges, simply move your Center *laterally* downhill to what will be the inside of the evolving turn. *With that move you are putting your body at the center of the turn.*

Your body is a box with legs, like one of those dancing cigarette packages that once graced television commercials. The box moves as a *unit* sideways; no twists of the hip, no dropping one shoulder as if you were an airplane banking—just move later-

---

*"Weight on the downhill ski" is one of the first dogmas of skiing (along with "bend the knees"). But in the carved turn the "downhill" ski is often uphill! Weight is carried on the uphill ski in anticipation of the turn, in which it will become the downhill ski. It is best then, in thinking of the skis in turns, to call them by the role they play in the turn. One ski is *outside* the curve of the turn, the other is *inside* the turn. Thus outside ski, inside ski.

ally downhill. The simplicity of the action is so difficult to accept we tend to decorate it, cluttering it with effort.

Here is the way we get the feel of the motion into our bodies in the off-slope sessions of the Centered Skiing workshops. Try it.

Stand in an open doorway, preferably a narrow one with a smooth jamb. Stand in the General Position on skis, knees flexed. (Keep the image of your body as a box with dancing legs.)

We will simulate a turn to the right. Withdraw the weight from your right foot, sensing the settling of it on your left. *Leave it there.*

Lean against the doorjamb with your right shoulder and your body on a slant. (Check to be certain you left the weight on your left foot and that your knees are still flexed. It might help to allow your right foot to lift slightly to make clear where your weight is.) Let your body register that position. Notice the banking of your shoulders. Notice that your hips are away from the wall. Notice just where on your left foot your weight is.

Still leaning with your shoulder, bring your right hip against the door too—nothing else changes. Register that position. Notice that your shoulders are now *level.* And notice how the weight has moved to the *inside* of your left foot.

Play with the variations of that position for a moment, sensing the changes. For instance, roll your knees toward the doorjamb against which the box of your body rests. Sense the increased pressure on the inner edge of your left foot.

Roll the knees outward, away from the jamb, sensing what changes that makes. Notice that the lower part of the body box must *twist* to accomodate that knee position. The pelvic region now no longer faces the way your feet are pointing, but off to the left. The line of your hips no longer shares the same plane as your shoulders.

But, more important, notice what that outward roll of your knees has done to the distribution of weight on your left foot. It has taken it off the edge and spread it more evenly over your entire foot. *If you were on skis, you would have flattened your ski and skidded out of your carved turn.*

Since it is necessary in a carved turn to have the maximum authority on the inside edge, then you can tell quickly from your doorway experiments that the best way to do that is (1) move your body as a unit (a box) *laterally* (not rising, not sinking, not tilting), hip and shoulder moving simultaneously to the doorjamb and (2) make certain that your hips or knees do not break to the outside of the turn (i.e., away from the doorjamb).

Stay with your doorway. Standing upright as before in the General Position as if on skis, withdraw the weight from your right foot so that you are standing on your left. Place your left hand on the outside of your hip and press it toward the doorjamb. Yield to the pressure, allowing your upper body to move to the doorjamb. The whole box goes without spilling a Rice Krispie—level, not tilted.

Allow the *feel* of that position to sink into your body. Your feet—the weight is clearly on the inner edge of your left foot. Your knees—they are flexed, indeed, your right leg hangs there like that of an old horse standing in the sun, and are pointed the direction your feet are pointing, or slightly toward the doorjamb. Your hips—the right side is against the doorjamb and both face the direction of the feet with no twist outward. Your shoulders—they are level and square with the rest of your body as they lean against the support.

Now let's make some *left* turns.

Stand as before with knees flexed. This time press your body toward the other side of the door. Experiment with that side, too, and see how the signals to your feet change with the tilting and the twisting. Now, in the level position, which puts more pressure on the inside of your right foot, let the feelings register in your body.

Now "link" some turns. Move from doorjamb to doorjamb letting your awareness touch on the withdrawal of weight from one foot, the lateral move to the door, and the squareness of knees and hip to the same plane as the shoulders. Now move back through the middle to the other side.

It helps, if you are not well padded, that the door be. A wall can be equally supportive, but you can only "turn" one way. Lacking door or wall you can always practice the movement mentally. Remember to move from Center, upright, square to your feet. Keep the weight on the inner edge of the appropriate foot (the right foot when you lean left, the left foot when you lean right).

You are carving, except for the snow.

• In carving a turn, maintain firm contact with the snow. To avoid skidding out of your carved turn and to control its radius it is important that a steady pressure be exerted on your skis (*ski,* really, since all functioning weight is on the inside edge of the ski on the outside of your turn).

It is with reason I say "a steady pressure be exerted" rather than "exert a steady pressure." Of course, *you* are doing it, but if you become too conscious of your agentry, there is a tendency to *do* something. The wrong circuits get plugged in and *effort* rears its head, and what you get is tension instead of pressure. Tension blocks the energy flow through the legs, and the feet go dead in the boots.

The pressure best comes from an image. Use either an image of that bowed C in the snow and your need to hold it there, or some metaphor that sets off the right responses. One that often worked for me was simply *ooze*. A steady inexorable flowing over the surface. In my orange ski suit I would say, "The Great Orange Ooze strikes again!" and then feel my legs extending where necessary to ensure that firm feedback from the snow's surface.

Tune into the energy flow. With your consciousness at your single-pointed Center, sense the *ch'i* as you breathe it in. Feel the course of the energy streaming downward to tie you to the earth; feel it through the feet and legs and along the pertinent edge. At the same time feel from your Center an upward, outward coursing of energy that links you with heaven. You are the conduit between heaven and earth. *T'ien ti.*

And in that sense, and that sense only, there is still "up-and-down" in the ski turn. It doesn't show, it just feels.

How much energy is in that flow to the skis (how much pressure you exert along with the cranking inward of the knees and the extremity of the body lean) determines whether one turn will have a shorter radius than another. With an easing of the pressure and a straightening of the knees, the little c's turn into large C's.

Ride the carve now, without a mistrustful flick of the hips. Your next turn is born in this one.

Is that, then, *the* way to carve a turn? No. No one skis just like anyone else. We have different techniques differently understood. We have different images, differently employed. We have different bodies, differently lived in.

Each skier is his own prototype.

My way of the carved turn, I have put together from my understanding of Sigi Grottendorfer's approach which I have gained working with him in the Centered Skiing workshops, and from my visual memory of his skiing—a poetic interplay of minimal curves in which one cannot tell the skier from the skiing.

Now forget everything and find your *own* way to carving.

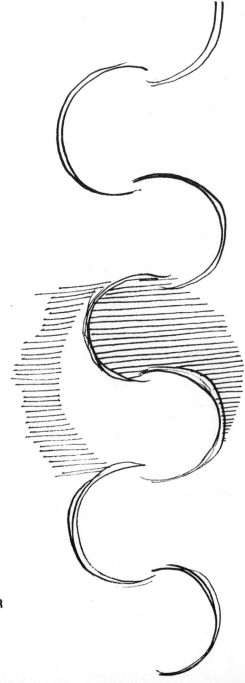

12

THE FIRST CHAPTER

I hate quotations. Tell me what you know.
— RALPH WALDO EMERSON

In this chapter are musings about things ranging from cold to equipment, from conditioning to bending at the waist. I had planned to fill the pages with cogent quotations such as: "Oak as tiny acorn knows already what's worth knowing,"* and leave your ears ringing with revelations. Then I ran across the Emerson line that opens the chapter. And so I will.

BENDING AT THE MIDDLE

A gross fault of beginning skiers has always been a tendency to fold at the middle. "Don't bend at the waist!" they are scolded. More advanced skiers are similarly warned when they ski bumps. Absorb the bumps from the feet upwards, they are advised, not

*R.G.H. Siu, *Ch'i, A Neo-Taoist Approach to Life.*

from the head downwards. A sure sign the advice has been ignored is their jackknifing forward, head in the vanguard. "Don't bend at the waist!"

But they are not bending at the *waist* at all; they are all bending at the *hips.*

Let's explore this matter of bending right now. Stand up. Bend your ankles forward and see what happens. You'll discover that your knees must bend, too. That is the source of the old piece of teaching wisdom: "Bend ze ankles not ze knees, and you will be a whiz on skis."

Now bend your knees *without* bending your ankles. You cannot do it without either hanging on to something or bending your body well forward to keep your balance. Let your body bend until it has taken on the squatting posture familiar to bunny hills the world over. Now scan your body to observe exactly *where* you are bending. You are bending at the knees, of course, and at your middle—but *which* middle? It is, please notice, at your *hips.* Your waist, that most middle of middles, is probably perfectly straight. If it isn't, straighten it, and leave only the bend at your other middle, your hips.

Now gradually move that bend upward from the hips to the waist and see what happens. Your pelvis cups under to contain your Center; your ankles and knees ease into a bend; your upper body is more erect; and your back—from your knees to your shoulders—is no longer as angular as a T square, but is now curved into a giant C. If you were on skis, you would be standing in a General Position pleasing to the most exacting by-the-book instructor.

Bending at the *waist* is not the villain of the piece after all; bending at the *hips* is.

Now that you realize that you have two middles at which to bend, experiment with them to see which does what. Stand erect and ceremoniously bow from the hips. Notice that you can do that with perfectly straight legs. Indeed, your knees want to lock in a backward arc. Now bow from the waist *alone,* breaking your body right at the belly button. Allow the rest of your body to do what it must do to accommodate the action. Notice that you can bend *right at the waist* with ease only if your knees and ankles soften and bend, too.

Let the sensation of that bending from the waist register in your body and spark an image by which you can remember it.

The image I got was of Portuguese oysters. Portuguese oysters are long, narrow delicacies with very rough shells which I seek out whenever I am in Europe at the Right time. "One bite and you're 20 fathoms down" is the way my friend Allen Eager used to describe them. When I squeezed a bit of lemon on them they contracted at the touch of those acidic drops. That's the image I use now—a few drops of lemon juice at my Center and my muscles seem to draw toward that point just like the oysters' contraction. My pelvis tucks under without *being tucked* under, my waist bends into a curve, my back rounds slightly, and my knees and ankles yield into a bending—all from that image of the oysters.

Now I can stop *trying not to bend* at the waist when I ski, because I know that such waist-bending has been mistakenly maligned. Nor do I need to *try not to bend* at the hips, because I also know that all such trying goes for naught, anyway. Now all I need to do is be a Portuguese oyster with a few drops of lemon juice at my Center, and I reflexively bend at all the right places.

☯

CONDITIONING AND DIET

I have failed to address myself to conditioning and diet in this book, not because they are not important, but because they are highly individual. Find what is best for you. It is true that if your muscles are not strong enough for the demands of skiing, your timing will be off, your stamina will suffer, and you will risk injury. It is true that if you are not flexible, you will bend less and break more.

A good training program will strengthen your muscles, improve your cardiovascular system, increase your flexibility, and improve your resistance to disease and malaise. A good training program is good not because it is good for you, but because you find it good. It works best when it is not imposed on you, either by others or by yourself.

Such an organic program of diet and exercise is not easy to come by and will take some searching on your part. The search is part of the program.

Some books on the subject are listed in the Appendix of this book; many others are in a compilation by Jim Polidora called "A Reader's Guide to the Biology of the Mind/Body" in the Autumn, 1977, issue of *Somatics* (a journal). Reprints can be ordered for a nominal fee from the author: Dr. Jim Polidora, PO Box 709, Davis, California 95616.

A book about stretching—not the bouncing, muscle-bunching type, but the cat-like giving yourself to gravity—published by its author and available by mail is called simply, *Stretching* (by Bob Anderson with Jean Anderson's drawings). The book is about stretching in general with specific stretching exercises for specific sports, skiing included (wall charts are also available). Order it $7, postpaid (38 cents more for California residents for tax) from: Stretching, PO Box 2734, Fullerton, California 92633.

A final note about conditioning: it doesn't have to hurt to count. Your range of muscle use is best extended by not forcing the limits; there is nothing inherently character building in pain.

ABOUT EQUIPMENT

I notice in some skiers a touch of what we used to call *Formula III mentality*. When I started racing cars there was a class of finicky little machines that were powered by modified motorcyle engines, all rear mounted—an oddity not everyone recognized as a portent of the future. These Formula III cars were driven by a special breed, inveterate tinkerers all. The race itself seemed incidental to them; they lived for technology. Most of us normals suspected that Formula III drivers were happiest when their cars broke down on the course—a not uncommon occurrence—and presented them with a Problem and an excuse for what they loved best: tinkering. Some skiers seem to share that penchant.

Don't understand me too quickly. I do not belittle the importance of suitable equipment. To realize your potential as a skier—indeed, even to enjoy skiing fully—your skis, boots, and poles should fit you physically and suit your characteristics as a skier. As my friend Doug Pfeiffer, columnist for *Ski* puts it, you should be "in tune" with your gear. Doug is right in saying that unless there is harmony your equipment will dominate you. Another way of being dominated by your equipment is by constantly fiddling with it.

You probably know skiers like some I know: every day a new theory and a new panacea, a new magic craftsman who is going to reshape their boots and their lives. Today add another strip of gaffer's tape to the right boot, remove one from the left, tomorrow add a wedge here, a shim there. Cant, then recant the canting. They are no longer merely concerned about their equipment; they are fixated on it.

When you get *stuck* anywhere on anything, and lose the rhythm of the part/whole relationship, the flow stops. Pull back a minute; free yourself from a simplistic linear notion of cause and effect and open your awareness to the kaleidoscopic interplay of influences. You may learn something about your relationship with your equipment.

Skiing styles obviously are affected by newly developed equipment. Ordinary skiers do things with today's skis and boots that they would not have dreamed trying 20 years ago. But equipment is influenced in turn by skiing styles. Many innovations in boots and skis follow a trail already broken by an innovative skier. For example, Jean-Claude Killy's unique way of skiing came first; then his coach Marcel Arpin worked with manufacturers to modify skis and boots to express the strengths of Killy's technique and that of the other members of the French team. Genius affects its tools beyond just using them well.

Once something is done—something that appeared to be dependent on design of the new equipment—a barrier is down. Oddly, what was not thought possible, or at least not thought *of* with the old equipment, can now be done with it, too. Equipment design proves to be instrumental, but not essential.

Let me call once more on the car world for an example. I am thinking of two incredible Finnish rally drivers, Timo Makinen and Rauno Altonen, who were on the British Motor Corporation (BMC) rally team the year I also drove for BMC in various European rallies. The pair, driving the little front-wheel-drive Mini Coopers, had perfected a cornering technique that was a marvel of precision on snow-covered or gravel roads.

The technique involved using the left foot on the brake and the right foot on the accelerator and playing those controls as if they were the pedals of a honky-tonk piano. Rather than *applying* the brake or the power in desired amounts they kept them both on fully and simply *decreased* the amount of each at appropriate moments by lifting the indicated foot the desired amount.

Thus they kept the front wheels clawing at the road surface with the right foot, and with the left foot (the brake) they controlled the angle at which the rear of the car slewed outward. This angle, of course, controlled the radius of the particular turn, with an accuracy impossible on icy mountain passes using ordinary steering techniques. It was the nearest thing to a carved turn you can do in a car. The two also made good use of the hand-brake turn, a maneuver that could quickly whip a car around 180° on a narrow road, or even 360°.

This was fairly radical suff some 15 years ago, and at first it was deemed practicable only in small front-wheel-drive cars, but its application spread. The next spring in Florida, Timo was at Sebring to race for BMC. He had a rented Cadillac for his off-course transportation, and I can still see that beige monster waltzing down an unused back road in linked 360°'s, Timo grinning broadly at the wheel.

The point of this is that the Cadillac would never have *suggested* the technique; the Mini did. But once the technique was established it was no longer *confined* to the original equipment. Be aware of this interplay between user and equipment and avoid getting stuck on either side. Remember, too, that the user/equipment relationship is like the chemistry of perfume; what one does for others it may not do for you.

In searching out ski equipment that best expresses your skiing or in tuning your equipment to harmonize with your skiing, you might find it helpful to keep certain things in mind: The Hawthorn Effect, Interfaces, Dynamics, and the Ecology of the Body/Mind.

The Hawthorn Effect. The name comes from Hawthorn, Pennsylvania, the site of a Western Electric laboratory in which researchers conducted experiments to determine what effect on producitivity such things as light and noise levels have. They found that even contradictory changes—either brighter *or* dimmer lights—had the same immediate effect: productivity increased. The element in the experiment that has come to be known as the Hawthorn Effect was the power of merely *doing something;* it's not what's done so much as that something is done.

I translate the Hawthorn Effect to ski equipment with the observation that *any* change tends at first to be perceived as an improvement. Move the binding forward a little, now back. Cant to the right, now left. Yeah, that's better; it's all better. The Hawthorn Effect is probably greater among the average recreational skier than ski racers. Racers usually have a more specific notion of what they want their equipment to do for them, but when a racer *is* subject to the Hawthorn Effect, the results can be disastrous.

If you as a skier do not possess a fine sensitivity to your equipment, comparable perhaps to a driver's noticing whether his tires are under or overinflated by a few pounds, then be wary of the Hawthorn Effect when you start your tinkering. It can keep you fiddling for seasons on end and leave you vulnerable to every self-styled expert in the lift line who will gladly see you through many generations of expensive equipment.

Interfaces. The best skiers will tell you that skiing all comes, finally, to feeling the surface of the snow. More is demanded of you as a skier than of the princess with the pea under nine mattresses. You must feel something as fugitive as snow through the involved thicknesses of your ski, your binding plates, and your boot soles. But *feel* of the snow is not really what you are after so much as *sense* of it. You tune into the snow more kinesthetically than you do tactilely, drawing conclusions about its texture, its temperature, and its resistance to passage based on how your feet interact with it.

You know where your foot is and what it is doing through constant messages from muscles, tendons, and joints relating to it. These messages compute out to a specific location and attitude of your foot. The more numerous and precise the messages are, the more complete is the picture in your control booth, and the more accurate and precise will be orders for future movements. All this is going on without your conscious surveillance. It is body thinking.

What you can do consciously to ensure adequacy of the two-way communication is remove any obstacles under conscious control. Clear the decks of unnecessary thinking. Banish inappropriate tension. Be aware of your feet and do not stop that awareness at your boots. Attend to the interface between your foot and the inside of your boot; be aware of it as a boundary, not a barrier. Send your awareness through your boot to where it touches your skis. Again, this is a boundary, not a barrier. Then go on to the interface of ski and snow, which is also a boundary and not a barrier, unless you let it become one.

Information must move freely for you to sense the snow and your relationship with it. It must not be blocked by barriers to the free flow of energy. The tension of *holding on* in the legs, in the ankles, and in the toes can erect barriers. Release those tensions. The well-intentioned excesses of your boots can build barriers, too. You need your full kinesthetic range unlimited by boots that are too stiff to allow your feet, ankles, and lower legs their tiny but critical cybernetic adjustments.

Dynamics. The body is not a structure; it is a process masquerading as a structure. The body is an enduring process; its functions are quicker processes in harmony with it. In a movement, such as the contraction of a muscle, "a quick and short process wave is superimposed on a long-lasting and slowly running wave," as Ludwig von Bertalanffy describes it.

Nonetheless, some ski boots are designed as if the body were a structure instead of a system of relationships. They are designed to strengthen a segment of that structure that appears too weak for some demands skiing makes on it. Take the super-stiff boot, for instance. It latches on to the desirability in skiing of limited lateral movement of the ankle and of having the weight forward rather than back on the skis, and then locks those ideals into a boot so rigid in construction that lateral movement of the ankle is virtually eliminated and straightening the ankle enough to stand normally is impossible. These boots, in effect, take a relatively slow process wave and freeze it, as a photograph freezes action.

Now, is that a good idea? It is a good idea to limit the lateral wobble in our ankles; it is a good idea to bend our knees and ankles. These boots *make* us do those things. But is it a good idea to *impose* a position on the body as if it were a statue? F.M. Alexander, in the quotation that opens Chapter 11, says, "There is no right *position,* but there is a right *direction."* His statement could not be more germane to skiing.

In a dynamic process change is most preservative of the system. Rigidity destroys. Fixity is death. In skiing it is the *getting* forward not the *being* forward that is functional. Constant tiny adjustments keep that forwardness, keep the energy flowing through the ski tips, and keep the knees bend*ing* not bent. Sometimes getting forward goes through a *sitting-back* phase, a dramatic moment that involves collecting energy backwards to be jetted forward in the skis before the body catches up. That moment is a photogenic one, which brings up another example of how stultifying fixity can be.

The high backs of the boots of the seventies, climbing up the calf like progressive ossification, were originally intended as a backstop against which racers rocked briefly as they accelerated their skis in a turn. Now the high backs have become sort of a candy-store wall where many young skiers hang out all the time. A valid use has jelled into a misuse. Entranced by the dramatic photographs of racers rocking back against their boot tops, these youngsters have taken what was a mere moment in a process and fixed it into a *posture.* It's as if they hoped to run the high hurdles by never getting out of the hurdle position. "Astride one does not walk," Lao Tzu said.

Another fixity of position has proved counter-productive in general use, also. This is the high interior wedge in the heels of many boots. The wedged heel tilts a skier forward rather like a Funny Car lining up at a drag strip. The exaggerated lift works well with specific skiers in specific situations, but generalized to the skiing public, the wedgie met with problems. In practice the extreme of the built-in forward lean called out for another extreme to moderate it—the skier's posterior, thrust backwards for balance.

Boots had altered rapidly from the above-the-ankle lace-up leather models to the mid-calf buckle-up plastic affairs that looked suitable for a soft landing on the moon. Apparently the extremes had been explored. By 1976 boots were changing again; by 1977, the change was a wave. Boots were getting lighter in weight, softer in construction—more flex, the ads said—with more attention paid to the interface of foot to boot. Feet were no longer dealt with as a mere connecting link to transmit knee movement to ski edge with the least loss of information, but rather as collectors, too, of valuable information, and performers of fine and important movements. The newer boots allowed the feet a more comfortable office with adequate insulation to perform their duties. The extremes of the elevated heel were moderating, too, with some boots going as flat as bedroom slippers.

The aspects of the super-stiff boot that had worked *with* the dynamics of the foot and ankle—like the improved lateral support—were not radically different, but those that had been interfering—jamming the important signals from the feet and imposing a rigidity where fluidity was preferable—were giving way. The way led to a more yielding, more neutral boot without loss of responsiveness.

Wine drinkers in this country talk dry and drink sweet. They want to be chic and they think dry is chic, but they also yearn for a little residual fruit sugar on the tongue. Vintners have learned to talk dry and sell sweet. Perhaps they have a lesson for ski-boot vendors. Skiers talk stiff and often buy that way; ski shops cater to their whim of having what the racers have. Many skiers unknowingly suffer for it; emprisoned in their stylish, colorful plastic, they ski as if shot with novocaine from the knee down.

If skiers bought softer they might find boots closer to what the racers look for, and they might be closer to that feel of the snow the racers talk about. My former neighbor, Rosi Fortna, when she was on the Olympic team, skied in junior boots, and her friend Penny Northrup raced in ordinary "ladies" boots. Even the present crop of racers, who have known nothing but plastic and super-stiff, do not choose boots that *overwhelm* their kinesthetic sensitivity; many recreational skiers do, and so do many junior hopefuls, in trying to emulate the racers.

The Ecology of the Body/Mind. It is difficult to think in wholes when we have grown up analyzing things into bits and dealing with them separately. When we go to a doctor with a painful shoulder we still expect the shoulder to be the center of attention (and wonder why the acupuncturist is needling our foot). Even those trained in holistic approaches find it hard to avoid the seduction of the obvious symptom.

So it is with tinkering with our boots and skis and poles. The tendency is to treat symptoms. Yet nothing can be corrected from the periphery inward, anymore than yachtsman would think of unkinking a rope from the end inward.

If you normally stand with a disproportionate amount of weight on the outside of your right foot, some will encourage you to "correct" it with a shim or two, much as you would put a book of matches under a wobbly table leg. Their point would be better made if you were a table. Static alignment works only in a static world. You do not live in one; you certainly do not ski in one.

Treating a symptom does not rid you of the anomoly; it merely chases it elsewhere. By "correcting" your right foot you may well have made your left knee more vulnerable to injury. Or your right hip. And so the effects of symptom tinkering spiral through the body. Be aware of that. Specialists in symptom treating may disagree. They have impressive expertise and apparent successes with their methods; I do not deny them. But I would prefer to be realigned functionally from the Center outward rather than the periphery inward. I would prefer rolfing to canting. Rather than be shimmed and braced I would rather be assisted toward an integrated body by a student of Feldenkrais, or guided to a better use of self by an Alexander teacher. They deal with the body as process with a sensitivity to its ecology, and I prefer that to a strictly mechanistic approach.*

---

*Brief descriptions and addresses of various bodywork techniques are in the Appendix.

Speaking of ecology, biologist and author Barry Commoner has formulated four succinct laws of ecology that are worth keeping in mind for all of your tinkering and being tinkered with.

1. Everything is connected to everything else.
2. Everything must go somewhere.
3. Nature knows best.
4. There is no such thing as a free lunch.

APOSTROPHES

What's left out is as important as what is there. In any language there is *elision,* the slurring or omission of letters or syllables. In written form the absence is generally marked with an apostrophe, but what's left out is still there in the meaning. To understand what's meant, one must understand what's missing.

The language of movement is no different; skiing has apostrophes, too. Racers leave out many intervening steps as they seek the fastest route downhill. They *elide* their turns into the shortest possible statements. Arcs of carved curves become segments so brief as to look like straight lines. Skis flash from edge to edge leaving out entire words. It is rapid-fire conversation in dialect, and beginners in the language are at a loss to follow it. Trying to copy it verbatim can lead to misstatements.

Advanced racers know in their bodies what was left out. What is visibly unexpressed is nonetheless there, within them, as an internal apostrophe. Younger racers must get the same meaning in their bodies, too. Before they can safely elide their turns like the experts, they must *dig* the apostrophes.

INDEPENDENT SUSPENSION

You, as a skier are a bifurcated animal, split from ground level almost to your Center. This split leaves two fully independent limbs that are suitable for a wide range of independent action. However, certain ski techniques have had a tendency to blur that independence and foster what I call the Mermaid School of Skiing. The mark of excellence in this school is that no daylight ever shows between the legs. In the turns, one knee is often tucked in behind the bend of the other so that the two act as one. The lower limbs are treated as if they were a single unit.

Not many ski schools still teach this technique, but its effects remain. The currently favored view is that a natural stance on skis, feet about hip width apart, is best. One boot enslaved to the other is no longer the mark of an accomplished modern skier; yet many skiers still harbor the notion that it is, and keep striving for the mermaid look.

The feet-together fetish has generated some interesting species, a common one being the knock-kneed skier. Some skiers could manage to keep their legs tightly together down as far as their knees, but below that their legs splayed out like a stepladder.

Paradoxically, treating your legs as if they were a single unit sets up forces that act to separate them; treating them as if they were independent sets up forces that act to draw them together — close, but not too close. Your skis tend to come together because of what else you are doing, not because you are forcing them together. The *what else* is: skiing free of undue tension, skiing balanced over your skis, and skiing with your functional weight on the outside of your turns — in short, skiing Centered.

Although tucking one knee inside the bend of the other in your turns might make you appear as a single brush stroke against the snow, it also interferes with the freedom of your knees to respond to terrain changes independently. The technique limits the range of either knee and blunts the niceties of adjustment. Your skiing suffers.

Allow your legs to find their own space and to operate independently within that space. Let them move contrapuntally to each other in harmonic balance without sacrificing their individuality.

See your legs as the independent suspension system on a Ferrari, for instance; each one acts independently to smooth out the variations of the terrain it encounters, thus not disturbing the balance and controllability of the whole. After all, automotive technology has borrowed your knee as an analog for absorbing shocks. If you are going to borrow back, borrow the best. Why ski with a solid axle?

COLD

Although it is sometimes hard to believe when the air is as keen as razor blades, cold is merely the absence of heat. You know this, of course, but *realizing* it can help you ski warmer. You do not *get* cold in the sense of acquiring it, anymore than a sponge acquires dry; you lose heat. Heat is the one with wanderlust; cold is a description of what is left behind. Keep this in mind when you dress for winter weather, and choose your ski boots and clothing accordingly.

I have owned ski boots that might have been made of copper, so efficiently did they hasten any warmth in my feet toward the great outdoors. Some modern boots are designed for warmth. Nor need fabrics rely any longer on bulk or weight to trap body heat; modern weaves and synthetics do a better job in lightweight comfort.

Dress your body as you would insulate a house. Exposed and thinly clad areas are like windows or gaps in the insulation. Heat pours out of them—especially to moving air. An uncovered head is like an undampered chimney; a surprising amount of your total body heat can be lost if you ski bareheaded. A hat, therefore, does more than keep your ears warm; it conserves heat in the rest of your body, too.

How cold or warm you feel cannot adequately be described by a thermometer reading alone. The radiance of the sun is perceived as warmth on your skin even though the air, which can be heated only by convection and conduction and not radiation, is at a low temperature. Thus you can sit comfortably wrapped in sunshine on the ski-lodge deck on chilly days if you are out of the wind. Wind velocity and relative humidity also determine how cold you feel. Recently, many weather forecasters have begun to include the expected *effective temperature* as well as the projected thermometer reading for the day. This is called the *wind-chill factor*. Pay it attention; an air temperature of 30°F with a stiff breeze can *in its effect* be as cold as a -30°F reading on a still day. Even on moderately warm days if a high wind steals enough heat from your body, you can be chilled, perhaps dangerously.

The perception of cold, then, is not strictly a matter of degrees, nor need it be tied rigidly to *any* exterior factors. We have within us, largely unexplored, an amazing capacity for regu–lating our bodily processes including adjusting our thermostats as we choose. Yogis do it with practiced ease. Autogenesis, a thera-py technique developed in the 1930's by German psychiatrist J.H. Schultz, teaches patients a process in which they send feelings of warmth to their extremities. Other self-hypnosis and mind con-trol techniques can be equally effective.

Most dramatic, perhaps, are the adepts in Tibet who can reportedly sit naked in the snow for hours, melting an area around themselves with their self-generated heat. In 1970 there were studies by Elmer and Alyce Green, biofeedback researchers at the Menninger Foundation, working with Swami Rama. The Swami demonstrated that he could raise and lower the temperature in his hand at will at a rate of some 4°F a minute. Furthermore, he could differentiate between two spots on his right hand a few inches apart and raise the temperature of one and lower that of the other until the two differed by 10°F.

We are neither so grandiose nor accomplished in our Centered Skiing workshops, but we do something more than merely talk about the weather. Visualization, the technique discussed in Chapter 7, is the key. Here is one way to use it: Build an imaginary fire in your Center and warm your *ch'i*. See the coals glow and the flames curl, and as you breathe to that rosy core collect the warmed energy and send it to every part of your body. Gradually let it radiate out from your Center. Feel the flooding warmth ease downward through your thighs into your calves and to your feet and toes. Feel the swell of comfort flare through your chest and spill into your arms and down into your fingertips.

During the first Centered Skiing workshop on a day that came straight from the deepfreeze, two of us were boarding the chairlift with the usual comments about the extremity of the cold and the coldness of our extremities. The irony of the moment struck me. "Hey," I said, my shoulders hunched to my ears, "this isn't the way I *tell* you to do it." Clearly it was time to put theory into practice as we rode the lift.

First, we let go of our shoulders, relaxed our jaws with the chattering teeth, and let the shivering stop. We were not suddenly turned to pillars of ice, so we deepened our relaxation, built our fires in our bellies, and sent our warmed *ch'i* through our bodies. My left ear lobe began to tingle, my hands seemed to swell in my gloves, and the communication lines to my feet were reestablished. "What's happening with you, Nancy?" I whispered, though why I whispered I don't know. "I'm getting warmer!" she whispered back.

As the chair topped a crest where wind often cuts a cruel swath, I actually unzipped my parka a few inches. It wasn't an act of bravado. Indeed, I seemed to be more an observer of the act than its instigator. I also observed that the wind was blowing at its best. I saw it stir the trees, I heard it in the cables, I felt it on my face; but I refused the gift of its chill.

When we reached the summit we were both marvelously warm and brimming with delight. "It really works!"

I've used a variety of visualizations since with similar success. A favorite is to put a sun in my solar plexus, an appropriate image for an advocate of solar heating. And sometimes I put a mundane infrared bulb, like those in motel bathrooms, over my head and let my shoulder blades bake.

Find the images that work for you, and you need never ski anything but warm again. However, don't neglect the earlier advice on choosing proper clothing and attending to the daily wind-chill factor. On particularly brutal days you should also have a companion check your face from time to time for the white spots of frostbite. This caution is not inconsistent; consider the old Sufi saying: "Trust in Allah, but tie your camel."

LEARNING FROM MOVIES

There is a risk in learning from still pictures because stills take the truth of a moment and, by fixing it in time, make a lie of it. Movies move and can be valuable in learning.

Movies to learn from are probably best short (10 or 15 minutes maximum) and without narration. They are best watched in a receptive mode with soft eyes, not analytically. They are best *soaked in* rather than *looked at*. Let limb teach limb, let Center speak to Center.

Movies, if you let them, have other lessons to teach. They teach the interplay of *yin/yang* and the usefulness of the useless. Consider that in any film you watch you are looking for half that time at a blank screen. If it were not blank, there would be no illusion of movement. With videotape, the scan of the lines is equally ephemeral. It is the constant interplay of absence and presence that is perceived as a steady state.

Muse, then, on the importance of silence to music, of stillness to movement, and of holes to architecture. Enclosed space has no value as a building without gaps for windows or doors. That brings us once again to the empty cup.

APPENDIX

The list of body-work techniques on these pages is far from complete, but it is representative. The author has experienced some of them, not all. Their inclusion here is meant merely as an aid to any search upon which the reader might wish to embark; that is all. The addresses are those available in September, 1977.

ALEXANDER TECHNIQUE

F. Mathias Alexander began developing his approach to the use of self some 80 years ago. His technique emphasizes the role of the muscles of the head and neck in ease in movement. Some Alexander work is now done with a single teacher in a group, but traditionally the Alexander technique involves a one-to-one gentle manipulation (such as a hand on the neck) directing the body/mind to a less effortful means of doing while inhibiting the *end-gaining* that causes tension. "My doing was my undoing," is a classic Alexander remark. Kinesthetic awareness is enhanced and old inefficient habits of movement are consciously replaced by new simpler ones.

Addresses: England

Society of Teachers for the Alexander Technique
3 Albert Court, Kensington Gore, London SW7, England

United States

American Center for the Alexander Technique:

New York   **142 West End Ave., New York, NY 10023**
San Francisco   **931 Elizabeth St., San Francisco, CA 94114**
Los Angeles   **811 23rd St., Santa Monica, CA 90403**

BIOENERGETICS and NEOREICHIAN TECHNIQUES

If the body reflects all emotional and psychological conflicts, then a way to deal with the conflicts is to deal with the *armoring* of the body—its muscular tensions and habitual attitudes. Bioenergetic techniques are aimed at freeing the self through freeing the body. More body-oriented than traditional psychoanalytic approaches, bioenergetics is more psychoanalytically oriented than other body-work techniques. Students of the controversial Wilheim Reich have modified his theories and evolved a variety of approaches of their own, all stressing the unity of body/mind and the importance of dealing with both at the same time.

Addresses of some of them:

Institute for Bioenergetic Analysis, Alexander Lowen
144 E. 36 St., New York, NY 10016

Center for Energetic Studies, Stanley Keleman
2040 Francisco, Berkeley, CA 94709

Core Energetics, John C. Pierrakos, MD
Institute for the New Age of Man
340 E. 57 St., New York, NY 10022

Radix (formerly Interscience), Charles Kelley
1611 Montana Ave., Santa Monica, CA 90403

ESALEN INSTITUTE and ESALEN SPORT CENTER

Workshops in various body-oriented approaches, including many of those listed below, are frequently scheduled at Esalen or in conjunction with Esalen elsewhere. A quarterly catalogue is available for $2 a year, a single inspection copy sent on request. Al Chung-liang Huang, Bob Nadeau, George Leonard and Mike Spino, all mentioned in the text of this book, often conduct workshops at Esalen.

Address: **Big Sur, CA 93920**

FUNCTIONAL INTEGRATION   Moshe Feldenkrais

There are two aspects to the Feldenkrais method; Functional Integration involves a one-to-one nonverbal manipulation of the body guiding it to a correction of specific anomalies; Awareness

Through Movement exercises devised by Dr. Feldenkrais can be done in groups or alone, with or without a teacher, since his books and tapes contain clear descriptions of his simple exercises. The exercises are verbally directed slow adventures in discovery leading to a greater awareness of body use, and the gradual elimination of redundant, superfluous, and contradictory movements.

In August, 1977, Dr. Feldenkrais completed a 3-summer course in his work in San Francisco and graduated 60 students. After a post-graduate session in 1978 in San Francisco, he will start a similar series of courses in New York in 1979. A list of those qualified in the Feldenkrais method will be made available to anyone requesting it.

Address: **Feldenkrais Guild**
1776 Union St., San Francisco, CA 94123

Feldenkrais Institute
49 Nachmani, Tel Aviv, Israel

LOMI METHOD

When the kings and queens of old Hawaii overindulged in poi, or so the story goes, they were further indulged with a massage called *lomi*. Under that name six people evolved a body/mind technique drawing on their assorted work with Randolph Stone (Polarity Therapy), Ida Rolf (Structional Integration), and Fritz Perls (Gestalt Therapy) and added aspects of *aikido* and meditation. Three of the six—Robert Hall, Alyssa Hall, and Richard Heckler—are still associated with the Lomi School, where they involve themselves with a holistic approach to education for living. Some Lomi practitioners are more strictly body-work oriented. A list of those trained to do Lomi work is available from the school.

Address: **Lomi School**
475 Molino Ave., Mill Valley, CA 94941

POLARITY THERAPY   Randolph Stone

Dr. Stone, a chiropractor, osteopath, and naturopath with a deep grounding in physics and ancient Oriental and Greek philosophy and health systems, drew on the entirety of his background to develop Polarity Therapy some 60 years ago. It is designed to balance the energy centers within the parts of the body and to balance the parts of the body with each other—the front with the back, the top with the bottom, and the left side with the right. Polarity Therapy has four aspects: (1) *manipulation* by the practitioner using his hands as bipolar contact points; (2) *exercise*, including stretching and energizing exercises particularly suitable for skiing; (3) *diet*, emphasizing a personal study to determine the effects of various foods on the individual at different times; and (4) *thinking*, fostering an awareness of the inseparability of mental attitude and physical well-being. *Balance* is the key word.

Dr. Stone, now nearing 90, retired in 1973 passing his torch on to Pierre Pannetier. Polarity Therapy literature and Dr. Stone's books are available through him. Besides practicing, Pannetier also trains therapists. *Depth of study* and *experience* are classic Stone watchwords.

Variations in the practice of Polarity Therapy have arisen. One difference is in the degree of force or pressure used in the manipulation aspect of the therapy. The San Francisco and Mill Valley groups listed below might be said to belong to a more gentle school, the Washington group to a "harder" school, although any such characterization can be misleading. All the addresses below are sources for therapists. The Washington group conducts 7-week-long training sessions and will furnish for the asking a list of graduates.

Addresses: **P. Pannatier Polarity Therapy
401 North Glassell St., Orange, CA 92666**

**Polarity Health and Education Center
of San Francisco
649 Irving St., San Francisco, CA 94121**

**Polarity Center of Mill Valley
10 East Blythedale, Mill Valley, CA 94941**

**Polarity Health Institute
PO Box 86, Olga, WA 98279**

SENSORY AWARENESS   Charlotte Selver, Charles V.W.
Brooks

Drawing on the teachings of Elsa Gindler and Heinrich Jacoby, Charlotte Selver developed the gentlest of all the body/mind techniques. It is a guidance toward *being*, a simple and direct experiencing without preconception. With her husband, Charles

Brooks, her health permitting, she gives workshops from Maine to Mexico. A new home base is planned for her by the Zen Center of San Francisco at their Marin County farm.

Address: **Charlotte Selver**
San Francisco Zen Center
300 Page St., San Francisco, CA 94102

STRUCTURAL INTEGRATION   Ida Rolf

Dr. Rolf, a biochemist by training, developed her theories and techniques over a period of 30 years. She believes in the plasticity of the human body and designed a system of ten hour-long sessions to free it from its prison built by habits and trauma, and restore it to the good graces of gravity. There is also a series of advanced work beyond the original set. All sessions involve one-to-one work in which the body is manipulated and deeply palpated by the practitioner.

The body's usually ignored connective tissue called *fascia* is the critical focus of the rolfer's fingers, knuckles, and elbows. Fascia sheaths the muscles. Through habitual misuse and abuse, physical and psychological, fascial tissue has become shortened, thickened, and stuck to the fascia of other muscle bundles, thus limiting the range of movement and experience. The rolfer probes deeply into the body to separate these adherences, and to stretch and lengthen the tissues and release the body to a more gracious alignment in gravity's field.

"You do not *have* a body, you *are* a body," is a frequently quoted Dr. Rolf statement. She has also said, "Word has been going around Esalen that Ida Rolf thinks the body is all there is. Well, I want it known that I think there's more than the body, but the body is all you can get your hands on."

Rolfers do get their hands on the body, and *in* it, often to a painful depth. Much is made of the pain of rolfing. There *is* pain, but it is a unique pain. It is not experienced as an *applied* pain, such as one might incur from a blow or a fall; it is experienced as a *stored* pain, one hoarded for lost reasons until its release by the rolfer. It hurts as it departs, searingly at times, and then it is gone. Relief settles in its place. Names and addresses of qualified rolfers are available on request.

Address: **Rolf Institute**
PO Box 1868, Boulder, CO 80306

STRUCTURAL PATTERNING   Judith Aston

Patterning was first developed by Judith Aston, a former dancer, to be used in conjunction with rolfing, enabling those who had been rolfed to make better use of the new length and ease of their musculature. It has evolved a life of its own. Patterning is a gentle direction, experienced one-to-one, leading toward a simpler, easier way of using the body. Judith Aston has worked with skiers, as well as many other specific groups, directing their awareness to better use of their bodies.

> Address: **Structural Patterning Institute**
> **PO Box 114, Tiburon, CA 94102**

TOUCH FOR HEALTH   John Thie

Dr. Thie, a chiropractor, has drawn on this chiropractic training as well as on osteopathic techniques, on theories of energy flow in the body from Dr. George Goodheart, and on applied kinesiology to come up with a holistic approach to keeping the body/mind in healthy balance. The method is taught at the Touch for Health Institute and described in Dr. Thie's book, *Touch for Health*. What one learns is a simple test to determine the relative strengths and weaknesses of the major muscles at a particular time, and how to balance them by, in effect, switching the weaker muscles back "on." Balancing the body this way before any strenuous physical activity, such as a day on the ski slopes, can help prevent injury as well as enhance performance.

> Address: **Touch for Health Institute**
> **1192 North Lake Ave., Pasadena, CA 91104**

BOOKLIST

Alexander, F.M.   *The Resurrection of the Body,* New York, Dell, 1971.

Anderson, Bob   *Stretching,* illustrated by Jean Anderson, Fullerton, Cal., Robert A. Anderson and Jean E. Anderson, 1976.

Anderson, James L., and Cohen, Martin   *The West Point Fitness and Diet Book,* New York, Rawson Associates Publishing, 1977.

Arguelles, Jose   *The Transformative Vision: Reflections on the Nature and History of Human Expression,* Berkeley, Shambhala Publications, 1975.

Arnheim, Rudolf   *Visual Thinking,* Berkeley, University of California Press, 1972.

Assagioli, Roberto   *The Act of Will,* an Esalen Book, Baltimore, Penguin Books, 1973.
———— *Psychosynthesis,* New York, Viking Press, 1971.

Barlow, Wilfred   *The Alexander Technique,* New York, Alfred A. Knopf, 1973.

Bateson, Gregory   *Steps to an Ecology of Mind,* New York, Ballantine Books, 1972.

Bertherat, Therese, and Bernstein, Carol   *The Body Has Its Reason: Anti-Exercises and Self-Awareness,* New York, Pantheon Books, 1977.

Brooks, Charles, V.W.   *Sensory Awareness: The Rediscovery of Experiencing,* New York, Viking Press, 1974.

Brown, Barbara   *New Mind, New Body — Bio-Feedback: New Directions for the Mind,* New York, Harper & Row, 1974.

Burnshaw, Stanley   *The Seamless Web,* New York, Geo. Brazilier, 1970.

Capra, Fritjof   *The Tao of Physics: An Exploration of the Parallels Between Modern Physics and Eastern Mysticism.* Berkeley, Shambhala, 1975.

Castaneda, Carlos *Journey to Ixtlan: The Lessons of Don Juan,* New York, Simon & Schuster, 1973.
———— *A Separate Reality: Further Conversations with Don Juan,* New York, Simon & Schuster, 1971.
———— *Tales of Power,* New York, Simon & Schuster, 1974.
———— *The Teachings of Don Juan: A Yaqui Way of Knowledge,* New York, Ballantine Books, 1974.

Chang Chung-yuan *Creativity and Taoism: A Study of Chinese Philosophy, Art & Poetry,* New York, Harper Colophon Books, 1970.

Chuang Tzu *Basic Writings,* translated by Burton Watson, New York and London, Columbia University Press, 1964.

Chuang Tsu *Inner Chapters,* a New Translation by Gia-Fu Feng and Jane English, New York, Vintage Books, Random House, 1974.

Daumal, Rene *Mount Analogue: A Novel of Symbolically Authentic Non-Euclidean Adventures in Mountain Climbing,* Baltimore, Penguin Books, 1960.

Deikman, Arthur *Personal Freedom: On Finding Your Way to the Real World,* New York, Grossman, 1976.

de Mille, Richard *Put Your Mother on the Ceiling: Children's Imagination Games,* New York, Penguin Books, 1976.

DeRopp, Robert *The Master Game: Pathways to Higher Consciousness Beyond the Drug Experience,* New York, Dell, 1968.

Dhiegh, Khigh Alx *The Eleventh Wing, an Exposition of the Dynamics of the I Ching for Now,* New York, Dell, 1974.

Downing, George *The Massage Book,* New York, Random House and Berkeley, The Bookworks, 1974.

Downing, Jack, and Marmorstein, Robert, eds. *Dreams and Nightmares: A Book of Gestalt Therapy Sessions,* New York, Perennial Library, Harper & Row, 1973.

Dubos, Rene *Mirage of Health: Utopias, Progress and Biological Change,* New York, Perrennial Library, Harper & Row, 1959.

Dychtwald, Ken *Bodymind,* New York, Pantheon Books, 1977.

Eliade, Mircea *The Myth of The Eternal Return or, Cosmos and History,* Princeton, Princeton University Press, 1974.
———— *Myths, Dreams and Mysteries: The Encounter Between Contemporary Faiths and Archaic Realities,* translated by Philip Mairet, New York, Harper Colophon Books, 1975.

Feldenkrais, Moshe   *Body and Mature Behavior: A Study of Anxiety, Sex, Gravitation and Learning,* New York, International Universities Press, 1966.
———*Awareness Through Movement: Health Exercises for Personal Growth,* New York, Harper & Row, 1972.
———*Awareness Through Movement, Learn to Learn: A Manual, and Recorded Lessons* (includes five audio cassettes), Pittsburgh, Westinghouse Learning Corp., Training Systems Division, 1975.
———*The Case of Nora,* San Francisco, Harper & Row, 1977.

Gallwey, W. Timothy   *The Inner Game of Tennis,* New York, Random House, 1976.

Govinda, Lama Anagarika   *The Way of the White Clouds: A Buddhist Pilgrim in Tibet,* Berkeley, Shambhala, 1970.

Granit, Ragnar   *The Purposive Brain,* Cambridge, MIT Press, 1977.

Gray, Henry   *Anatomy, Descriptive and Surgical,* Philadelphia, Running Press, 1974.

Guenon, Rene   *The Reign of Quantity and The Signs of the Times,* translated from the French by Lord Northbourne, Baltimore, Penguin Books, 1972.

Gunther, Bernard   *Sense Relaxation Below Your Mind,* New York, Collier Books, 1968.

Gurdjieff, G.I.   *All and Everything: Beelzebub's Tales to His Grandson, Books 1, 2, 3,* New York, E.P. Dutton, 1973.
———*Meetings With Remarkable Men,* London, Routledge & Kegan Paul, 1963.
———*Views From the Real World,* New York, E.P. Dutton, 1975.

Hall, Edward T.   *Beyond Culture,* Garden City, N.Y., Anchor Press/Doubleday, 1976.
———*The Hidden Dimension,* Garden City, N.Y., Anchor Books/Doubleday, 1969.

Harding, M. Esther   *Psychic Energy: Its Source and Its Transformation,* Princeton, Princeton University Press, 1973.

Herrigel, Eugen   *Zen in the Art of Archery,* New York, Pantheon Books, 1953.

Huang, Al Chung-liang   *The Living Tao,* Menlo Park, Cal., Celestial Arts, 1976.
———*Embrace Tiger, Return to Mountain: The Essence of T'ai Chi,* Moab, Utah, Real People Press, 1973.

Huizinga, Johan   *Homo Ludens: A Study of the Play-Element in Culture,* Boston, Beacon Press, 1972.

Ichazo, Oscar   *Arica Psychocalisthenics: The Arica Institute's Original Program of Exercise and Meditation,* New York, Simon & Schuster, 1976.

Ingham, Eunice D. *Stories the Feet Can Tell: "Stepping to Better Health,"* Rochester, N.Y., Ingham Publishings, 1975.

Jacobsen, Edmund *Progressive Relaxation,* Chicago, University of Chicago Press, 1929.

Jaynes, Julian *The Origin of Consciousness in the Breakdown of the Bicameral Mind,* Boston, Houghton Mifflin, 1977.

Johnson, Don *The Protean Body: A Rolfer's View of Human Flexibility,* illustrated by Charles Ramsburg, New York, Harper Colophon Books, 1977.

Jones, Frank Pierce *Body Awareness in Action: A Study of the Alexander Technique,* New York, Schocken Books, 1976.

Jung, Carl *Man and His Symbols,* Garden City, N.Y., Doubleday, 1964.

Kapleau, Philip, ed. *The Three Pillars of Zen: Teaching, Practice, and Enlightenment,* Boston, Beacon Press, 1967.

Keen, Sam *Voices and Visions,* New York, Perennial Library, Harper & Row, 1976.

Koestler, Arthur *The Act of Creation: A Study of the Conscious and Unconscious in Science and Art,* New York, Dell, 1973.
————— *The Ghost in the Machine,* Chicago, Henry Regnery, 1967.
————— *The Roots of Coincidence: An Excursion Into Parapsychology,* New York, Vintage Books, Random House, 1972.

Koichi Tohei *Aikido in Daily Life,* Tokyo, Rikugei Publishing House, 1975.
————— *Book of Ki: Co-ordinating Mind and Body in Daily Life,* Tokyo, Japan Publications, 1976.

Kostrubala, Thaddeus *The Joy of Running,* Philadelphia and New York, J.B. Lippincott, 1976.

Lao Tzu *The Tao te Ching.* Following are some of the many translations and commentaries:
————— Wu, John C.H. Asian Institute Translations #1, New York, St. John's University Press, 1961.
————— Lau, D.C. Middlesex, England, Penguin Books, 1963.
————— Waley, Arthur *The Way and Its Power,* New York, Grove Press, 1958.
————— Chan, Wing-Tsit *The Way of Lao Tzu,* New York, Liberal Art Press, 1963.
————— Chang Chung-yuan *Tao: A New Way of Thinking,* New York, Harper Colophon Books, 1975.
————— Suzuki, D.T., and Carus, Paul, tr. *The Canon of Reason and Virtue,* LaSalle, Ill., Open Court, 1974.
————— Feng, Gia-Fu, and English, Jane, New York, Vintage Books, Random House, 1972.
————— Tao Te Ching, translated by D.C. Lau, Baltimore, Penguin Books, 1963.

Lee, Linda   *Bruce Lee: The Man Only I Knew,* New York, Warner Paperback Library, 1975.

Leonard, George   *The Ultimate Athlete: Re-Visioning Sports, Physical Education, and the Body,* New York, Viking Press, 1975.

LeShan, Lawrence   *How to Meditate: A Guide to Self-Discovery,* New York, Bantam Books, 1975.

Leuchs, Arne, and Skalka, Patricia   *Ski with Yoga,* Matteson, Ill., Greatlakes Living Press, 1976.

Levi-Strauss, Claude   *From Honey to Ashes,* New York, Harper & Row, 1973.
————— *The Savage Mind,* Chicago, University of Chicago Press, 1966.

Lilly, John   *The Center of the Cyclone: An Autobiography of Inner Space,* New York, Julian Press, 1973.
————— *Programming and Metaprogramming in the Human Biocomputor: Theory and Experiments,* New York, Bantam Books, 1974.

Lowen, Alexander   *The Betrayal of the Body,* New York, Collier Books, 1972.

Luce, Gay   *Body Time,* New York, Bantam Books, 1973.

McKim, Robert H.   *Experiences in Visual Thinking,* Monterey, Cal., Brooks/Cole, 1972.

Maisel, Edward, ed.   *The Alexander Technique: The Resurrection of the Body: The Writings of F. Mathias Alexander,* New York, University Books, 1970.

Maslow, Abraham H.   *The Farther Reaches of Human Nature,* an Esalen Book. New York, Viking Press, 1975.
————— *Toward a Psychology of Being,* New York, D. Van Nostrand, 1968.

Masters, Robert, and Houston, Jean   *Mind Games: The Guide to Inner Space,* New York, Viking Press, 1972.

Metzner, Ralph   *Maps of Consciousness,* New York, Collier Books, 1971.

Miller, Dr. Emmett E.   *Selective Awareness,* 2 Frederick Court, Menlo Park, CA 94025, self-published, 1975.

Murphy, Michael   *Golf in the Kingdom,* an Esalen Book, New York, Viking Press, 1972.

Naranjo, Claudio and Ornstein, Robert   *On the Psychology of Meditation,* New York, Viking Press, 1972.
————— *The One Quest,* New York, Ballantine Books, 1973.

Nideffer, Robert M.   *The Inner Athlete: Mind Plus Muscle for Winning,* New York, Thomas Y. Crowell, 1976.

Ornstein, Robert E.   *The Nature of Human Consciousness: A Book of Readings,* San Francisco, W.H. Freeman, 1973.
———— *The Psychology of Consciousness,* New York, Viking Press, 1972.

Ouspensky, P.D.   *In Search of the Miraculous,* New York, Harcourt, Brace & World, 1949.
———— *A New Model of the Universe: Principles of the Psychological Method in its Application to Problems of Science, Religion and Art,* New York, Vintage Books, Random House, 1971.

Perls, Frederick S.   *Ego, Hunger and Aggression,* New York, Vintage Books, Random House, 1969.
———— *In and Out the Garbage Pail,* Lafayette, Cal., Real People Press, 1975.
———— *Gestalt Therapy Verbatim,* New York, Bantam Books, 1971.
———— Hefferline, Ralph, and Goodman, Paul   *Gestalt Therapy,* New York, Julian Press, 1951.

Pirsig, Robert   *Zen and the Art of Motorcycle Maintenance,* New York, Bantam Books, 1975.

Prestera, Hector, and Kurtz, Ron   *The Body Reveals,* New York, Harper & Row, 1976.

Ram Dass, Baba   *Be Here Now,* San Cristobal, N.M., Lama Foundation, 1971.
———— *The Only Dance There Is,* Garden City, N.Y., Anchor Press/Doubleday, 1974.
———— ,and Levine, Stephen   *Grist for the Mill,* Santa Cruz, Cal., Unity Press, 1977.

Reich, Wilhelm   *Character Analysis,* New York, Farrar, Straus & Giroux, 1949.

Reps, Paul, comp.   *Zen Flesh, Zen Bones: A Collection of Zen and Pre-Zen Writings,* Rutland, Vt. and Tokyo, Charles E. Tuttle, 1957.

Rolf, Ida   *Structural Integration: The Re-Creation of the Balanced Human Body,* New York, Viking Press, 1977.

Rosa, Karl Robert   *You and At: *Autogenic Training — The Revolutionary Way to Relaxation and Inner Peace,* New York, Saturday Review Press/E.P. Dutton, 1973.

Roszak, Theodore   *Unfinished Animal: The Aquarian Frontier and the Evolution of Consciousness,* New York, Harper & Row, 1975.

Samples, Bob   *The Metaphoric Mind: A Celebration of Creative Consciousness,* Reading, Mass., Addison-Wesley, 1976.

Samuels, Michael, and Bennett, Harold   *The Well Body Book,* New York, Random House and Berkeley, The Bookworks, 1973.

——————— *Spirit Guides, Access to Inner Worlds,* New York, Random House and Berkeley, The Bookworks, 1974.
——————— and Samuels, Nancy *Seeing With the Mind's Eye: The History, Techniques and Uses of Visualization,* New York, Random House and Berkeley, The Bookworks, 1975.

Schutz, William *Elements of Encounter,* Big Sur, Cal., Joy Press, 1973.

Shah, Idries *Caravan of Dreams,* Baltimore, Penguin Books, 1968.
——————— *The Sufis,* New York, Anchor Books, Doubleday, 1971.

Shaw Robert, and Bransford, John, eds. *Perceiving, Acting and Knowing,* Hilldale, N.J., Lawrence Erlbaum Assoc., 1977.

Sheehan, George A. *Dr. Sheehan on Running,* Mountain View, Cal., World Publications, 1975.

Singer, June *Androgyny: Toward a New Theory of Sexuality,* Garden City, N.Y., Anchor Press/Doubleday, 1976.

Siu, R.G.H. *Ch'i: A Neo-Taoist Approach to Life,* Cambridge, Mass., The MIT Press, 1974.
——————— *The Man of Many Qualities: A Legacy of the I Ching,* Cambridge, Mass., The MIT Press, 1968.
——————— *The Tao of Science: An Essay on Western Knowledge and Eastern Wisdom,* Cambridge, Mass., The MIT Press, 1957.

Smith, Adam *Powers of Mind,* New York, Random House, 1975.

Spino, Mike *Beyond Jogging: The Innerspaces of Running,* Millbrae, Cal., Celestial Arts, 1976.

Stapleton, Ruth Carter *The Gift of Inner Healing,* New York, Bantam, 1977.

Stevens, Barry *Don't Push the River: (It Flows by Itself),* Lafayette, Cal., Real People Press, 1970.

Stevens, John, O. *Awareness: Exploring, Experimenting, Experiencing,* Moab, Utah, Real People Press, 1971.

Stevens, John O., ed. *Gestalt Is—A Collection of Articles About Gestalt Therapy and Living...,* Moab, Utah, Real People Press, 1975.

Tart, Charles T. *States of Consciousness,* New York, E.P. Dutton, 1975.

Tart, Charles, ed. *Altered States of Consciousness: A Book of Readings,* New York, John Wiley, 1969.

Thie, John F., with Marks, Mary *Touch for Health: A Practical Guide to Natural Health Using Acupuncture Touch and Massage to Improve Postural*

Balance and Reduce Physical and Mental Pain and Tension, Marina Del Ray, Cal., DeVorss, 1973.

Tutko, Thomas, and Tosi, Umberto   *Sports Psyching: Playing Your Best Game All of the Time,* Los Angeles, J.P. Tarcher, 1976.

Watts, Alan   *Tao: The Watercourse Way,* with Collaboration of Al Chung-liang Huang, New York, Pantheon Books, 1975.
———— *The Way of Zen,* New York, Pantheon Books, 1957.

Weil, Andrew   *The Natural Mind: A New Way of Looking at Drugs and the Higher Consciousness,* Boston, Houghton Mifflin, 1972.

Welch, Holmes   *Taoism: The Parting of the Way,* Boston, Beacon Press, 1966.

Westbrook, A., and Ratti, O.   *Aikido and the Dynamic Sphere,* Rutland, Vt. and Tokyo, Charles E. Tuttle, 1974.

White, John, and Fadiman, James, eds.   *Relax: How You Can Feel Better, Reduce Stress, and Overcome Tension,* New York, Dell/The Confucian Press, 1976.

Wilhelm, Richard, tr.   *The I Ching* or *Book of Changes.* Princeton, Princeton University Press, c. 1950, 1967.

Witherell, Warren   *How the Racers Ski,* New York, W.W. Norton, 1972.

THE AUTHOR: Denise McCluggage, flatlander born (Kansas), discovered skiing while at Mills College in Oakland, California. Nonetheless she was graduated Phi Beta Kappa and embarked on a journalistic career, then known as the newspaper business. She worked at the San Francisco Chronicle before migrating east and becoming motor sports and skiing editor of the New York Herald Tribune. Known for doing what she wrote about, she skied, parachuted, bobsledded, and raced cars with her greatest successes in a Ferrari. She was considered one of the two or three best women drivers in the world, winning rallies and races from Monte Carlo to Sebring. She now supports her whims by writing, photographing, designing and conducting workshops. She lives in Vermont with Hathaway, who is spending this life as a calico cat.

THE ARTIST: Bill Brauer flunked high school art. Thus encouraged he launched a career of drawing to a different drummer. His commissions range from a painting "in the manner of van Eyck" on a harpsichord lid and soundbox to etchings for a poetry book and designs for stained glass windows. Primarily a printmaker, his work is in several permanent collections. He is working on a series of etchings on a grant from the Vermont Council on the Arts. New York born, he lives in Vermont where he teaches and tends to his farm menageries from ducks and pigs to sheep whose wool he shears for a resident weaver, his wife, Judy Fox.

THE BOOK: The Centered Skier was set in Optima with Helvetica chapter titles by Northlight Studio Press, of Barre, Vermont and printed (on 60 pound Supple Offset natural by Bergstrom) and bound by Essex Publishing Company, of Essex Junction, Vermont. The book was designed by the author. Jim Dodds designed the cover title for Bill Brauer's painting and assembled the mechanicals.